The Algorithmic Analyst

Mastering NLP For Modern Intelligence

Zhao Xintong

Global East-West. London

Contents

The New Frontier

Information Overload and the NLP Imperative in Intelligence

Modern Intelligence Information Overload Overview

Every intelligence agency is presented with both challenges and opportunities due to the increasing digitisation of the world. The nascent opportunities of data spur to surging technology, communication, and information sharing infrastructure. At the same time, there are boundless social media outlets along with sensors augmenting data, which breach conventional intelligence methods and flood them with information overwriting previously amassed intelligence data in legacy big data vaults. Intelligence professionals equipped with modern technology are operating in the profoundly transformed information landscape in hopes of streamlining actionable intelligence. Foreign intelligence agencies now face the ever-present dilemma of expeditiously extracting data-driven insights from relentlessly amplifying torrents of information. Traditional analytics techniques are taking the brunt of increasing volume, velocity, and variety of big data seen, and falling behind adaptive innovation, rendering structural analytical enhancement desperately necessary. Further augmenting processes are oceans of unstructured documents, reports, multimedia, emails, and texts to name a few. Retaining from bytes of text needs analysing alongside compiling action items like drawing analytical diagrams while navigating through data retention pills. It is the sheer sea of rampant, unfiltered data and perceived overload rendering natural processing language the pipette narrows beacons of modern intelligence.

With the aid of NLP technologies, intelligence agencies can now automate the tedious processes involved in sifting through and extracting insights from enormous amounts of unstructured text data. NLP can help relieve some of the burdens posed by voluminous unstructured data, providing agencies with opportunities for enhancing their analytical prowess. While the intelligence community is faced with the staggering challenges posed by vast amounts of data, they also stand to benefit from an unprecedented chance to delve into intricate global phenomena. NLP as well as other modern technologies enable intelligence agencies to generate intelligence in a timely manner, reduce the effects of information congestion, and serve the intelligence needs of decision-makers at the precise moment when the information is most critical. Chapters that follow will focus on more complex issues of the deluge of data in modern intelligence and examine the challenges posed by advanced NLP technology.

Challenges and Opportunities Posed by Big Data

The emergence of digital information has profoundly transformed the processes associated with intelligence gathering and analysis. There is at once an opportunity and a challenge for an organisation to leverage big data due to its volume, velocity, and variety. One of the main concerns that information technology poses is making it possible to collect, curate, store, and analyse data from different and distant sources. The traditional collection methodologies are increasingly becoming obsolete since there is an immense amount of information generated in the contemporary world. The risk of critical information being under or over-collected because it's simply too rapidly generated and complex is real. Further, the enormous amount of disparate, unstructured data complicates the extraction of useful information within a reasonable timeframe for human analysts. Beneath these difficulties, however, there are prospects for technological and innovative advancement. Enabling patterns, trends, and connections to be identified which were formally unrecognisable — big data holds the potential to yield valuable insights with the right methodologies, frameworks, and tools.

Moreover, the application of more sophisticated analytics, machine learning, and natural language processing (NLP) continues to foster the emergence of intelligent systems that can process vast amounts of data and aid in the efficiency of intelligence operations.

The combination of structured and unstructured datasets provides thorough cross-sectional data for more descriptive and integrative analysis. Treating big data as a strategic asset rather than a challenge requires strong leadership in information governance frameworks, scalable system architectures, and the development of sophisticated world-class analytics capable of harnessing the boundless possibilities offered by this exceptionally data-rich environment. Intelligence agencies are best positioned to confront, and thus leverage, the challenges and opportunities posed by big data, requiring agencies to rethink their approach and adopt advanced and bespoke technologies and techniques aligned to the contours of contemporary information infrastructure.

Technological Advancements and Their Impact on Intelligence Gathering

In this last decade, advancements in technology have completely changed the world of intelligence gathering. The new forms of digital communication, social media, and the sheer volume of information available on the internet have drastically increased the amount and type of data available for analysis. Data collection has become increasingly complicated as agencies are faced with a number of new challenges as a result of an influx of data; this includes automation, complex evolving international relations, and new governance warnings. In one sense, overwhelming amounts of information may hinder the understanding of ever-evolving global issues, but from another perspective, robust technologies are available that can be used to transcend the evolving barriers in gathering covert and actionable intelligence on global threats. As mentioned before, one of the more notable consequences of technological innovations is the increased use of natural language processing (NLP) in intelligence gathering. Analysts are able to take advantage of NLP systems to automate the processing and analysis of vast amounts of text, discovering intricate patterns that would normally go unnoticed because of how advanced and automated those dealing with intelligence data systems have become. Also, the introduction of advanced machine learning algorithms has permitted intelligence services to build sophisticated predictive models, allowing them to deal with anticipatable omnipresent risks more nimbly and accurately.

The amalgamation of geospatial intelligence, open-source intelligence (OSINT), and sentiment analysis through natural language processing (NLP) has made it easier to grasp global affairs and understand the sentiments of different populations. Besides, the development of deep learning and neural network designs has further refined the intelligence gathering capabilities by performing anomaly detection on intricate multidimensional datasets. All advancements have far-reaching ethical concerns and privacy implications where personal data collection and analysis wades into sensitive territories of individual privacy and data protection. While moving forward with the contemporary framework of intelligence gathering, it is vital for the agencies to grapple with these ethical dilemmas and, at the same time, make use of ever-evolving technologies. In a nutshell, the consequences of modern technologies on intelligence gathering are profound with the need to rethink the procedures of intelligence collection, its handling, and the use of technology to safeguard national security and counter multifaceted global issues.

Defining the Role of Natural Language Processing in Modern Intelligence

Natural Language Processing (NLP) systems have become increasingly recognised as foundational technologies of contemporary intelligence because they transform the methods through which information is obtained, processed, and analysed. Specifically, NLP assists intelligence agencies to extract value from the huge volumes of unstructured data which permeates the modern world's digital ecosystem. Through the application of computational linguistics, machine learning, and AI, NLP enhances analysts' capabilities to detect and extract patterns, sentiments, and relationships in text data which further improves the efficiency of intelligence analytic operations. In the scope of contemporary intelligence, the functions of NLP remain important for numerous reasons. First, NLP helps retrieve essential actionable intelligence from a multitude of sources ranging from open-source and social media to intercepted conversations, encrypted communications, and texts. With the use of named entity recognition, information extraction, and sentiment analysis, NLP allows data and text analytics to be performed on vast datasets with accuracy and speed to capture important entities and events, and also estimates and signals of interest and concern. Besides, NLP aids in translation and cross-lingual communication overcoming the hurdle of languages so that important intelligence will be accessible and can be acted upon universally and promptly.

NLP's advantages in data processing include predictive analytics and trend analysis, which allow intelligence agencies to foresee possible threats and opportunities. NLP processes with advanced algorithms and models aid in the recognition of shifting narratives, ideological shifts and potential security threats which assist in strategic planning. Its fusion with other sophisticated technologies like machine vision and speech recognition extends its intelligence domain relevance and usefulness. Given the current challenges faced by intelligence agencies regarding the realities of today's information environment, NLP remains fundamental in the quest for complete situational awareness, immediate response capabilities, and active risk avoidance. All the same, it is axiomatic that the use of NLP in intelligence work demands tight ethical boundaries focused on bias risks, privacy violations, and misuse of the technology. Thus, alongside setting the boundaries for the use of NLP in modern intelligence, ethical policies such as transparency and strained engagement must be upheld to ensure that harnessing its transformative potential remains aligned to societal expectations and legislative frameworks.

Comparative Analysis: Traditional Methods vs. NLP-Driven Approaches

An intelligence analyst has to depend on manually sifting through text data to generate actionable intelligence using traditional intelligence analysis methodologies, which is highly inefficient. The work done by human analysts is unmatched in terms of its intellectual heft, yet it continues to confront a veritable flood of competing information streams, rendering the work unparalleled but undertime. With information expanding exponentially, profound lags emerge in its extraction and synthesis into actionable intelligence, and every fragment of new data becomes invaluable. NLP driven approaches, on the other hand, bring an unprecedented change in how unstructured data is analysed and understood by intelligence agencies. Active machine learning and NLP systems, employing modern linguistic algorithms and pattern recognition, enhance automation in the extraction of relevant pieces of information from open source reports, social media data, as well as from intercepted transmitted information. With such advanced techniques, critical entities, events, and sentiment trends can be identified quickly without the risk of getting buried beneath a mountain of information. One of the most noteworthy advantages of NLP driven approaches is overcoming multilingual barriers which have previously slowed down intelligence operations by allowing real-time processing and analysis of multilingual documents. It is NLP driven methods that are necessary for detecting complex contextual nuances as well as enhanced connections between two or more pieces of information thus deepening and broadening the intelligence related details provided.

Unlike typical approaches that utilise manual encoding, deep learning, and keyword-based systems, NLP-powered techniques use named entity recognition and sentiment analysis to extract contextual information. Intelligence products created using NLP approaches are often more accurate and granular when compared to more traditional approaches, resulting in better decision-making and advanced threat detection. Based on the findings from this analysis, it is clear that NLP approaches have transformed intelligence analysis through automation due to the unmatched precision, accuracy, and profundity they bring in deriving crucial information from the vast pools of unstructured data.

Case Studies: Success Stories of NLP Implementation in Intelligence

Natural Language Processing (NLP) has proven highly beneficial in different operational areas within the field of intelligence. Through studying cases from different intelligence agencies, we can understand to what degree NLP can augment information extraction, analysis, and decisions in agencies. One of the most interesting case studies involves the counter-terrorism operation where NLP algorithms were employed to extract enormous amounts of data from open sources. Using enhanced entity recognition and sentiment analysis, the community was able to identify and preemptively thwart the attack. This demonstrates clearly the value of NLP in preemptive risk management. Another success story involves organised crime where sophisticated networks were uncovered with the use of document clustering, cross-document event and topic modelling. These technologies provided a means for law enforcement agencies to alleviate criminal syndicates and community-endangering activities. Furthermore, NLP powered machine translation has transformed multilingual intelligence analysis by fostering communication and collaboration across nations.

The utilisation of LLMs in the assimilation and evaluation of foreign language materials has remarkably accelerated the retrieval of pertinent intelligence information, crucially enhancing the effectiveness of international diplomatic activities and counterintelligence operations. The integrative case studies elaborate the outstanding prospects of NLP in modifying the processes and functions of intelligence operations beyond their conventional confines and bestowing exceptional power upon the intelligence analysts to obtain vital information, predict threats, and defend national security.

Key Tools and Technologies in NLP for Intelligence Applications

Natural Language Processing (NLP) has transformed intelligence workflows for most organisations, as they can now retrieve insights from unstructured data. To facilitate NLP's true possibilities in intelligence functions, it is important to know what tools and technologies are essential to its execution.

Named Entity Recognition (NER), one of the technologies which assists in NLP for intelligence, is critical in recognising and classifying named persons, organisations, places, dates among other entities. Intelligence analysts are able to piece together relevant information and describe relationships among different entities by completing entity-based classification and recognition. Additionally, tools for Sentiment Analysis are very useful in examining public feedback and detection of some shifts in sentiments which must be noted as they may possess some underlying important events, intrigues, or risks.

There are algorithms for document clustering and topic modelling that assist in summarising and structuring large corpuses hence helping analysts work their ways around massive amounts of data and spotting unusual data trends.

The availability of Machine Translation Tools have enhanced the analysis of foreign language content in intelligence agencies as they can scan materials in different languages with greater ease, implementing cross-lingual intelligence methods; there are no longer language barriers.

Capabilities such as query processing, context understanding, multi-modal information integration, among others, are sophisticated functions provided by Large Language Models (LLMs). Additionally, putting NLP-powered document summarisation tools to good use is extremely helpful in cutting down long texts into shorter documents retaining all key points, thus, providing more insightful summaries while also saving time and effort for intelligence analysts.

The merge of human experts and AI systems requires both parties to work together to find an ideal solution simultaneously. For this reason, there is a shift towards supporting Explainable AI which allows analysts to understand the logic of NLP models, thus, fostering AI trust. Simultaneously, new developments in Data Labeling and Annotation platforms facilitate the training of NLP models for intelligence domain data, thereby improving the effectiveness and trust placed upon AI intelligence solutions.

There is no denying the fact that modern technology alongside the growing need for advanced analytical capabilities has put the intelligence and science sectors at an advantage, equipping them with tools to evolve AI. Nevertheless, shifting the focus from theory to practice without a proper strategy can widen gaps between intelligence agencies working in the fast-paced world of modern intelligence. Therefore, risking failure without the right informed guidance.

Collaboration between Human Analysts and AI: Bridging the Gap

In the field of intelligence operations, the collaboration of human analysts with artificial intelligence (AI) systems is increasingly important for solving the challenges posed by modern data analysis. Whereas NLP systems (Natural Language Processing) AI capabilities scan vast amounts of unstructured data and process it with incredible speed, human analysts complement the lacking elements by providing critical thinking skills, industry knowledge, and context. Here, we look at the balancing act of harmonising their capabilities to achieve synergy and optimise the intelligence analysis workflow.

The defining attribute of any collaboration is the integration of AI powered NLP tools into the workflows of human analysts. This integration requires the creation of designer NLP Interfaces and dashboards that allow the analysts to work with them as easily as they do with any conventional windows application. A culture of continuous improvement and staff development which relaxes rigid hierarchies to raise human analyst skills to the levels requisite to NLP technologies is also required. Empowering human analyst pedagogy by teaching them the details of algorithms, methods, and best practices of NLP enhances collaborating with AI systems greatly.

One of the intricacies of this problem is establishing trust and transparency for both parties involved when transitioning to AI from human driven processes.

To address the worries emanating from the various algorithms composing AI systems, it is essential that the outputs of AI systems be placed within explainable, auditable, and human verifiable frameworks. These systems must allow for human input so that there can be additional integrations and AI biases mitigated through human analyst insights. Active collaboration should be incorporated into transcripts generated through NLP systems so that at every available stage, there is an improvement which contributes towards the intelligence gathering.

Another collaborative dimension that emerges between human analysts and AI that is often disregarded is the ethical angle. Privacy issues surrounding data, bias perpetration, and the use of NLP technologies all come into play. Strengthening oversight structures into the interplay between human analysts and AI ensures these technologies are used within legislation is a must. Addressing frequent impacts as well as creating regulations corresponding to these topics would give humans stronger control in the mix of AI usage. By attending to all these issues, the back and forth between humans and AI will be strengthened.

The collaborative prowess of humans and AI in intelligence operations can be utilised to reach the peak of flexibility. In their quest to provide urgent and precise intelligence, committed AI systems and human analysts can unlock sophisticated and deeply hidden insights out of complex and interwoven narratives.

In order to remain at the forefront of swiftly developing challenges and possibilities, it will be crucial to foster an integrated alliance between human thinking and computerised systems as technology continues to transform the strategic intelligence paradigm.

Strategic Implications of NLP in Intelligence Operations

Considering the maturity of Natural Language Processing (NLP), it is necessary to keep the strategic aspects in mind, especially from the perspective of its use in intelligence operations. With NLP, intelligence institutions can harness unstructured data, text, to produce actionable insights and assist in decision making. One major strategic advantage NLP provides is enhancement of situational awareness through the monitoring and analysis of multifarious sources, in real-time, like social media, news articles, and OSINT. With this, intelligence analysts can keep pace with newly emerging threats and rapidly changing environments. Automation of consistent tasks such as information triage, document summarisation, and analysis of other content in different languages, enables the NLP systems to do the grunt work, and allows human analysts to put their cognitive skills to use in more demanding tasks, increasing productivity through NLP technology. Use of NLP technologies helps intelligence institutions improve their information allocation and optimise resource management, increasing the efficiency and effectiveness of their operations. Moreover, NLP assists in uncovering patterns, connections, and trends in large datasets, which aids in reconsideration of possible risks and opportunities. All these advanced capabilities enable comprehensive strategic forecasting, threat assessment, and geopolitical analysis with far greater precision and agility which encompass analytic value.

Moreover, sentiment analysis and opinion mining based on NLP technologies can provide insightful information regarding public sentiment, political stability, and social unrest which would enable proactive action among policymakers and strategic decision-makers. Another critical impact NLP contributes to intelligence activities is the fight against disinformation, misinformation, and propaganda. With sophisticated linguistic scrutiny and anomaly detection, NLP technology can help identify harmful information, news, and influence campaigns that undermine honest information circulation with the aim of protecting information integrity and strengthening democratic resilience. The use of NLP equally raises strategic issues related to cyber security and privacy because the handling of sensitive textual information requires strong safeguards on data protection and compliance with ethical standards. Adapting to an ever-changing information warfare and hybrid threat environment requires intelligence agencies to fully implement NLP technologies into their operational planning. Additionally, collaboration and cross-border cooperation in NLP research and its application is indispensable in solving issues of global security and advancing the use of linguistic technologies responsibly in intelligence operations. With globalisation, the strategic impact of NLP is numerous, and must therefore amend policies, practices, and training frameworks to eliminate risks while maintaining ethical norms.

Conclusion and Future Directions: Preparing for the Evolving Landscape

The impact of natural language processing (NLP) in intelligence operations may mark the beginning of a new era in the manner information is acquired, processed, and analysed. Infusing AI techniques into data acquisition, analysis, and dissemination processes of intelligence information is a further challenge that agencies will have to meet. In the course of our discussion regarding NLP's integration into its intelligence applications, we have not yet touched upon issues that will emerge and await attention in the wake of ongoing technological progress. On the one hand, the ever-advancing technology presents endless possibilities, while on the other, the sheer volume of available data poses challenges for intelligence agencies. NLP, as a transformative technology, needs to be leveraged while considering its ethical implications and potential biases.

Accountability, trust, and reliability are essential factors sought by almost all domains. As NLP systems are employed in intelligence operations, addressing these factors demands collaboration with experts from various fields. This spans creating partnerships with linguists or domain specialists, employing data scientists, and providing oversight to assure these tailored NLP solutions meet prerequisites envisioned for intelligence analysis rigor. The intelligence community, and those outside it too, sustain normatively positive attitudes only when relations are transparent in their development and deployment processes. Agile and robust frameworks must be established while engaging human monitoring blended with AI-powered NLP systems to make intelligence outputs unquestionable.

The call to create vehicles for cross-language and cross-culture interoperability of NLP systems is growing alongside increasingly preferential paradigm shifts towards constructing cross-systems. The need deepens with the accompanying increase in workload and variety in task performance types due to ongoing intelligent industrial shifts.

Resolving global security issues will require multilingual NLP as it will allow intelligence agencies to penetrate different languages and glean information from a multiplicity of sources. In addition, the development of explainable AI and interpretable NLP models will allow analysts to understand and reason as to why automated NLP works the way it does, thus improving the scrutiny of intelligence outcomes.

Additionally, staying vigilant for emerging disruptive trends will be important for intelligence practitioners in the future. Whether it be the acceptance of multimodal data sources, quantum computing, or even ethical issues posed by synthetic media, intelligence agencies should be swift and flexible in their use of NLP. A focus on continuous learning and an open-minded culture will ease the tackling of complex issues on NLP, geopolitics, and global security matters.

To summarise, the fields of reasoning or NLP details within intelligence offer fantastic proficiencies and potentials. Responsibly aiding these outlets fills gaps towards smarter, trustworthy outcomes within intelligence aims on linguistic technologies.

Through these efforts, the evolving landscape of intelligence can be steered with strategic foresight, ethical integrity, and a steadfast commitment to the common good.

2

Foundations of NLP
Core Concepts and Terminology for Analysts

Introduction to Natural Language Processing

The function of Neural Natural Processors is important for enhancing Automated Body Language Recognition Systems because it allows the automation of the extraction, interpretation, and understanding of human languages. With the continued growth of social media, news articles, reports and personal communication, there is a colossal amount of unstructured text data produced every day. NLP systems can equip intelligence analysts, providing them with the right tools to manage and utilise information in various fields including decision making on matters pertaining to national security, law enforcement, intelligence, and business. The importance of NLP in analysing verbal human interactions as an intelligence analyst is equally important when it comes to extraction and recognition of human speech patterns. The sentiments and emotions associated with human interactions also support the recognition and identification of patterns and irregular behaviours that may possess unique strategic importance. NLP helps analysts convert unstructured text into structured data which can be cleaned, processed, and analysed, thus improving the efficiency and precision with which information is used and reducing interpretation redundancy. Moreover, NLP simplifies the multilingual text analysis problem. Language is no longer a limitation to the collection and analysis of information from different countries.

Within the field of intelligence analysis, this capability is important for tracking international trends, interpreting regional subtleties, and generating complete situational awareness. With the ongoing progress in NLP, particularly with the implementation of large-scale deep learning and multimodal methodologies, there are now unlimited possibilities for applying NLP in intelligence analysis. NLP's ability to process human language enables analysts to transcend outmoded practices of keyword searches and manual coding, allowing for sophisticated automated textual analysis at unprecedented volumes. Employing NLP not only streamlines the processes of intelligence analysis, enhances accuracy, and deepens some advanced non-human cognition linguistic patterns, but also explores intricate cognitive patterns, sentiments, and implications beyond human analytical abilities.

Theoretical Underpinnings: Linguistics and Knowledge Representation

As with any other academic or industrial discipline, the study of language, linguistics, is the backbone of Natural Language Processing (NLP) because it provides the necessary theories that enable language data to be analysed and processed. Here, we address the assumptions of Basic Linguistics that warrant the NLP practitioner's understanding of the hierarchy of language, its meaning, and usage including pragmatics. From the point of view of language, the subfields of its study include phonetics and phonology, morphology, syntax, semantics, as well as pragmatics. All these disciplines for NLP analysts need to be much more than simply fundamental so that they can create solid models of languages and process texts in natural languages. Besides, representation of knowledge is critical in NLP because it helps in the capture and organisation of semantic information in the text documents. So the development of sophisticated natural language processing systems that would need to interpret unstructured documents and extract meanings requires knowing how concepts are represented and structured by knowledge. Concepts such as ontology, semantic networks, or knowledge graphs can represent sophisticated interrelationships and conceptual structures which enable NLP algorithms to work with an enormous amount of textual data and extract meaningful insights from them.

We also discuss the relations between linguistics and knowledge representation, focusing on the interplay of linguistic theories with computational methods used in NLP. By bridging these domains, analysts comprehend better how linguistic theories can be turned into computation techniques which facilitate breakthroughs in language understanding and generation. Further, we need to investigate the implications of linguistic and knowledge representation theories in real-world NLP applications focusing on their relevance in dealing with problems like disambiguation, polysemy, and other forms of semantic ambiguity. With some understanding of linguistic principles and knowledge representation, analysts can improve their skills in applying NLP to rapidly evolving intelligence context and language processing for deeper analysis using sophisticated techniques and therefore become more innovative in intelligence analysis and beyond.

Tokenisation and Text Preprocessing Techniques

NLP workflows begin with tokenisation and text preprocessing. Tokenisation breaks down the text to a certain level that can be analysed further, features carved out—and this can be done at the word, subword, or character level. Different approaches exist for tokenisation such as whitespace based, rule based, or more advanced sentencepiece and byte pair encoding for subword tokenisation. Each approach has its own set of advantages and drawbacks, and the choice of tokenisation method often depends on the specifics of the NLP task at hand. After tokenisation, text data goes through text intervention techniques to cleanse and normalise the data. This step handles punctuation, special characters, case handling, stemming and lemmatisation, and other common language forms. Preprocessing also tackles removal of already defined terms, spelling, and untidy datasets.

Downstream NLP activities such as information extraction, sentiment analysis, or machine translation hinge on the quality of preceding steps, which must be designed and executed with precision. Furthermore, while deep learning algorithms and large language models have brought to the forefront the need for effective text preprocessing to achieve target performance metrics, very little effort has been put into the design and evaluation of text preprocessing in deep learning algorithms. The influx of new techniques to the NLP marketplace makes the development of new approaches for tokenisation and text preprocessing extremely important for effective language processing and generation. Following specific criteria during tokenisation and text preprocessing equips NLP systems to address various linguistic challenges, thus increasing usability and reliability in practical scenarios.

Word Embeddings and Semantic Representations

The development of word embeddings is an important aspect in natural language processing (NLP) because it allows words to be represented in a word vector. Word embeddings enable NLP systems to grasp the semantic relationships and contextual information of words, standing in the semantic similarities and context information situated between various words in numerous

NLP tasks. Distributed representation is a word's context and inference clue. Popular word embedding techniques such as Word2Vec make use of neural network models to learn an array of words from enormous text corpora. Global Vectors for Word Representation (GloVe) is another method which derives word vectors using global statistics of co-occurrence counts within a corpus. Algorithms not only comprehend individual words but relationships among them too due to the rich semantic information word embeddings capture. In a language, semantic representations aim at capturing the meaning of phrases, sentences, and even words thereby going beyond the syntactic structure. They help reduce ambiguity and assist in understanding context-dependent meanings. Converting text information into semantic representations enables NLP models to comprehend the essence of the language, improving the efficiency of its analysis. Moreover, semantic representations are essential in document classification, sentiment analysis, and machine translation because they need the sense of words. The science of word embedding and semantic representation is still being researched, with scientists trying to capture more elaborate details of meaning in an attempt to enhance NLP performance. As NLP develops, from unstructured text information, more profound information will be unlocked by word embeddings and semantic representations.

Part of Speech Tagging: Breaking Down Sentence Structure

One of the fundamental tasks in natural language processing is part of speech tagging, which is crucial in framing sentences conceptually and semantically deciphering text. As the name suggests, each word in a given sentence is assigned a part of speech which includes a noun, verb, adjective, or adverb. This forms the foundation for ontological linguistic investigation, thus supporting a well-rounded comprehension of the sentence architecture that is, its syntax. The precision accuracy of such pre-formed tagging techniques will impact subsequent steps in NLP applications like sentiment analysis, identifying named entities in texts, or even machine translation.

To determine the probable part of speech that fits contextually for a certain word within a sentence, different approaches such as rule-based models, statistical models, or deep learning methods are applied in POS tagging algorithms. While rule-based models centre around specific grammatical bounding boxes, statistical models learn from large annotated corpora to estimate the probability distribution of words with their respective POS tags. More advanced, recurrent neural networks and transformers have more recently shown superiority in part of speech tagging due to their ability to learn complex relations and contexts using deep learning architectures.

POS tagging deals with the problems of ambiguous polysemous words, out-of-vocabulary terms, and inflectional and irregular morphological variations of languages. As a result, scholars focus on novel ways to improve the precision and robustness of POS tagging for different languages and diverse systems and contexts while using linguistic knowledge, cross-lingual transfer learning as well as domain-specific modifications.

Fine-grained POS tagging is a new development alongside traditional sequential tagging that captures detailed morphosyntactic and deeper linguistically informed annotations and components. The extra detail aids comprehension of syntax, dialectal and intra-linguistic variation and phenomenon, aiding downstream applications and linguistics. Also, it has great importance in multilingual natural language processing (NLP) since the number of languages with unique grammatical complexities adds extra dimensions of difficulty that need specific treatment.

To summarise, Part of Speech tagging is an essential tool for linguistic analysis as well as Natural Language Processing, enabling advanced systems to parse, derive meaning, and extract pertinent information from the given text. It is cross-disciplinary work which expands the boundaries of applied language and enriches intelligent natural language processing systems and tools, language untangled from the sheer technological marvel.

Syntax vs. Semantics: Parsing Techniques in NLP

Within the context of Natural Language Processing (NLP), parsing techniques are essential for understanding the layered intricate meaning and structure contained within textual documents. Assigning meaning to texts requires two basic components: syntax along with semantics, which serve as the basis of parsing methods in NLP. Syntax covers the fields of grammar, word order, and sentence construction, whilst semantics focuses on meaning and context interpretation. The gap between semantics and syntax is what parsing techniques in NLP seek to address, and bridging these two gaps makes it easier for machines to understand human languages. Parsing, as a form of syntactic analysis which constitutes one of the core functions of parsing, seeks to break down phrases and sentences into basic structural elements: nouns, verbs, adjectives, prepositions, and many others. This process is critical in defining and understanding relations between words. Also, beyond the borders of syntax, parsing includes also some elements of semantic analysis where the meaning and interpretations of the words or phrases are assessed. The aim of semantic parsing is to uncover the meaning and hidden relevance contained within texts so as to enable a better understanding of messages. There are several approaches in

NLP to parsing, including but not limited to: rule-based parsing, statistical parsing, and parsing based on neural networks.

While rule-based parsing utilises specific grammatical rules to evaluate the structure of sentences, statistical parsing uses probabilistic models to deduce semantic and syntactic relationships. Parsing based on neural networks employs artificial neural networks to dominate the intricate patterns and associations of language. As NLP technologies advance, the complexity of natural language has prompted the emergence of hybrid parsing systems that integrate syntax and semantics. These hybrids seek to incorporate the best features of parsing driven by syntax and parsing driven by semantics. Furthermore, dependency parsing, a subset of parsing techniques, seeks to identify and describe the syntactic dependencies between words in a given sentence, focusing on how the various parts relate to each other. Along with the evolving parsing techniques, deep learning and computational linguistics are reshaping the field of NLP, which is leading towards more sophisticated models of parsing. The combination of syntax and semantics gives more understanding to language and serves many uses such as in extracting information, developing a question-answering system, and performing sentiment analysis. In the end, the importance of human-machine interaction and intelligence in modern society relies on the advanced parsing techniques in NLP.

Named Entity Recognition (NER): Identifying Key Information

Named Entity Recognition (NER) is one of the key tasks in natural language processing which deals with detecting, classifying and recognising entities in the free textual content. An entity may relate to a person's name, an organisation, a geographical place, date, number, or any other contextually significant word or phrase. In terms of significance, NER is very important in intelligence evaluation because it helps in extracting important intelligence from the texts.

Usually in NER, machine learning tools and some linguistic rules are applied in order to process the text, recognise, and classify the relevant entities. This process first requires the recognition of already Named Entities which then will be classified into such groups as person's name, company name, place, and so forth. The performance of NER systems has a direct relationship to the effectiveness of information extraction as well as knowledge discovery in the area of intelligence evaluation because they are usually relied upon for the accuracy of the components of intelligence.

In addition, NER is very important for the automating processes for enriching knowledge graphs and structured databases. Because of accurate tagging of elements analysts are able to use linked data models for critical data which enhances their retrieval. Such a system can greatly improve decision making as well as comprehensive intelligence and estimates and even intelligence reporting.

In NER, challenges include dealing with ambiguous references, entity disambiguation, recognition of multi-word entities. These problems require more sophisticated approaches to NER, such as the use of contextual information, heuristic domain models, and well-calibrated models. Moreover, the cross-linguistic variation of NER illustrates its relevance in multilingual intelligence tasks.

To conclude, the effective use of Named Entity Recognition allows analysts to quickly pinpoint and harvest vital pieces of information from various texts. With further developments in the field of NLP, it's nearly certain that NER technology will reshape the world of intelligence analysis by offering revolutionary methods for parsing and distilling insights from an immense volume of unstructured data.

Sentiment Analysis Fundamentals: Understanding Emotional Contexts

Effective communication relies heavily on emotions, and sentiment analysis is a crucial aspect in the field of natural language processing that involves capturing these feelings from texts. Traditionally, sentiment analysis refers to determining the emotional undertone of a text piece. It plays a significant role in diverse fields such as secondary data collection, social media analytics, and reputation management. From the perspective of intelligence analysis, emotional contexts surrounding textual data can unlock critical insights related to public sentiments, threats, and global relations. This module focuses on the core principles and practices of sentiment analysis to provide analysts with adequate competencies to use emotional cues in their work interpret and leverage emotional signals. Sentiment analysis is based on the assumption that every language reflects sentiments or feelings in wording, phrases, and contextual hints. The goal of sentiment analysis technology is to ascertain the general inclination of the text by classifying it as positive, negative, or neutral. The procedure includes both lexicon-based methods involving sentiment dictionaries and machine learning approaches where models are developed to detect emotions in trained datasets. Further, this module addresses the issues of sarcasm, irony, and cultural factors in sentiment analysis, highlighting the contextual meaning of interpreting sentiments.

The ethics of managing emotionally sensitive data and dealing with biases within sentiment analysis models are discussed, underscoring the analysts' burden of ethics in the sociotechnical system that incorporates emotions. Ultimately, proficiency in sentiment analysis equips analysts with the ability to detect attitudes and opinions in a multitude of sources which deepens the intelligence collected and improves its accuracy.

Machine Learning in NLP: Supervised and Unsupervised Approaches

Machine learning is a key component with respect to how computers can analyse and understand natural language text with meaning behind it. Here we consider the two branches of machine learning which are supervised learning and unsupervised learning in the context of NLP focused problems. Supervised learning entails training a model with labelled data. The algorithm used in machine learning in this case learns how to use the data provided and produce the anticipated results. In NLP, this may be illustrated by named entity recognition, sentiment analysis, or even document classification. Text corpora are created with the specific purpose of training models and algorithms such as SVMs, Naive Bayes, and Neural Nets among others. In contrast to supervised approaches, unsupervised learning includes all approaches in which a model tries to construct relationships or discover patterns in a collection of objects that have no labels. This phenomenon can be very helpful in capturing the underlying structures in text and discovering groups of documents or topics that share a lot of commonalities. Common unsupervised NLP applications are topic modelling, word embedding and clustering algorithms like

K-means and hierarchical clustering.

As noted earlier, the selection between supervised and unsupervised methodologies usually hinges on the specific NLP activity and the labelled data on hand. We will analyse the challenges, benefits, and complications of each with greater focus on the tangible implementation issues, revealing practical application problems. Understanding both approaches will enable analysts and practitioners to make effective use of machine learning technologies in their NLP tasks and improve the precision, speedy execution, and sophistication of the intelligence analysis.

NLP Evaluation Metrics: Assessing Model Performance

Considered within the context of NLP, model evaluation is one of the crucial stages in the development and implementation of any model. Evaluation metrics or benchmarks to assess the performance of an NLP model differ with tasks such as sentiment analysis, named entity recognition, machine translation, among others. Evaluation of performance is critical; however, the chosen metrics must depend on the primary purpose of the NLP system and its manipulated linguistic data.

Accuracy is one of the most traditional metrics used to evaluate NLP models, defined as the ratio of predicted instances to total instances evaluated. While accuracy gives an overview of performance, it can prove insufficient in the case of skewed datasets or in situations where different kinds of errors have differing weights.

Two very significant metrics that are precision and recall are always used with accuracy. Precision refers to the ratio of accurately predicted positives to the total number of predicted positives, whilst recall refers to the ratio of true positives to total positives. These metrics become more helpful in tasks with far greater consequences for either false positive or negative detections, for instance in extraction of information or recognition of entities.

F1 score, or the F-measure, is a hybrid metric that weighs precision and recall and provides a single value capturing both elements. This is particularly helpful in situations where a balanced combination of both precision and recall is needed.

As with any process, there are distinct evaluation measures tailored for particular subtasks in NLP. For example, in the case of machine translation, the BLEU (Bilingual Evaluation Understudy) score is employed widely to evaluate the translated text against human-produced translations. Symmetrically, in sentiment analysis, metrics such as mean squared error or cross-entropy loss compute the divergence between predicted and actual sentiment scores and are utilised.

Moreover, the growing intricacy and NLP model's multifaceted nature is motivating many to search for more novel measures aiming at evaluation that go beyond the traditional metrics. This includes the attempts to measure robustness of a model using adversarial evaluation and bias and fairness in metrics measuring language processing.

To sum up, the performance of an NLP model is assessed using multi-dimensional evaluation metrics rather than flat accuracy benchmarks. In crafted language tasks, the impact of errors is significant, therefore demands attention. With a blend of bespoke and generic metrics, analysts and developers have enough information to evaluate the models accurately with the selection and refinement of models.

3

Identifying the 'Who, What, Where, When'

Entity Recognition and Information Extraction

Introduction to Information Extraction in Intelligence Analysis

Data processing in information intelligence demands that unstructured information be processed and transformed into structured information systematically. This change will, however, require streamlining vast datasets arising from reports, social media posts, news articles, television broadcasts, among other dynamic and unstructured sources. Named entity recognition (NER), which in this context refers to identifying and labelling specific entities, plays a critical role in simplifying the categorisation of data into predefined classes such as people, organisations, locations, dates among others. With NER, intelligence analysts can decode the who, what, where, and when cloaked in extensive documents to unveil insightful underlying intelligence.

Information extraction is one of the cornerstones to effective intelligence analyses to be conducted. Unstructured data often contains rich patterns waiting to be exposed if only the right techniques are used. For example using NER, data can be organised leading to better targets, relationship comparisons, recognition of dependencies, interdependencies, and other trends that were not visible at first. Such phenomena not only help better organise stratified data but also enhance better understanding of the core reasons for correlating data points in order to formulate better analyses and objective prompts. Additionally extracting and recognising roles of key entities such as events, organisations and persons will aid intelligence professionals gain better understanding and trim vague intelligence gaps to build a clearer orchestrated intelligence.

Moreover, information extraction specifically facilitates advanced model and tool development, especially in this time of increasing data volume and velocity. Through NER and similar methods, professionals in charge of intelligence can set the groundwork for the next analytical tasks such as sentiment analysis, network analysis, and event forecasting. To put it differently, information extraction helps analysts discover actionable insights and provides timely, insightful evaluations by enabling analysts to tap into the concealed value within unstructured data.

The gap identified in intelligence operations emphasises the need for a more advanced NER driven tool to address the problem of information extraction in modern intelligence practices. The acceleration of changes in global politics, as well as emerging information systems, make the rapid and precise recognition of critical entities and interrelations increasingly important in raw text. Addressing the gap in information extraction solutions empowers analysts to connect disparate pieces of information, turning them into significant intelligence, therefore offering a decisive advantage in the constantly evolving environment of modern analytical intelligence.

The Role of Named Entity Recognition (NER) in Structured Data Analysis

Named Entity Recognition (NER) is particularly important to structured data analysis in the field of intelligence and security. Its main job is to detect and classify key unstructured elements in a given text, be it name of a person, organisation, place, date or some numerical data. NER enhances the productivity of information analysis by automating the extraction and classification of these entities where an analyst need not manually search through endless files of information. NER is more or less an essential component in the intelligence analysis for automated recognition and classification of core pieces of information that frames the complete story.

NER also helps produce entity knowledge graphs depicting the relationships among the various entities and their attributes. Such knowledge graphs help in discovering the intricate relations, trends and networks that are often hidden in the data. Besides, NER aids the construction of timeline analyses by identifying temporal references together with the chronological order which helps in the contextualisation for reasons relating to investigation and prediction.

As noted, the consequences of NER go beyond the extraction of data, as it is the groundwork for more complex analytical processes like sentiment analysis, disambiguation, and even trend spotting. The integrity and trustworthiness of downstream analytic processes hinges on the discerning and classifying of entities done by NER with high precision and recall rates. There is a growing trend in the enhancement of NER systems to contextual and semantic understanding so that they may capture meanings and disambiguate references within several contexts due to the evolution of NLP technologies. Therefore, NER's relevance in structured data analysis is foundational and at the same time adaptive, responding to the many changes and intricacies of language with constant evolution in the intelligence field.

Methods and Approaches: Supervised vs Unsupervised Techniques

Employing supervised or unsupervised techniques presents a critical consideration for information extraction intelligence analysts. Each technique carries a unique set of advantages as well as challenges that impact the effectiveness of extraction accuracy. In supervised techniques, systems trained on annotations of patterns and features in the provided training dataset are able to perform recognition and extraction of entities with a higher accuracy. In contrast, unsupervised techniques do not use labelled data in their work and often rely on statistical and/or clustering methods within the unstructured text to figure out, extract and classify the entities. The choice of either of the two approaches entails a deep understanding of the dataset, the task complexity, and the available resources. Supervised techniques perform well in cases where labelled training datasets are available, yielding high accuracy; however, they are constrained by the lack of extensive training datasets, domain specific, or ever-changing entity types. On the contrary, unsupervised techniques are not restricted by labelled training data and allow for the open use of different text sources, and are capable of adapting to new entity types. While this type of approach is advantageous, the reliance placed on statistical patterns can lead to the undue influence of noise, demanding a greater amount of supervision than in guided methods to achieve an equivalent degree of precision.

Analysts of intelligence have to carefully evaluate the trade-offs of accuracy, scale, and agility, especially in regard to their chosen methods of information extraction. Furthermore, blending supervised and unsupervised techniques into hybrid frameworks has become increasingly popular as a way to capture the strengths of both approaches while offsetting their weaknesses. These novel amalgamations often use the initial supervised models to bootstrap unsupervised learning, so that precision is borrowed from supervised methods, but the flexibility of unsupervised methods is preserved. With the rapid pace of change in the discipline, the search for newer and more powerful methods of information extraction continues, focusing on radically new approaches, as well as building on existing ones to enable intelligence analysis with maximum precision and depth.

Entity Linking and Disambiguation: Enhancing Contextual Understanding

The techniques of entity linking and disambiguation are crucial processes for improving the contextual understanding and the accuracy of information extraction in the domain of intelligence analysis. Information within unstructured data often contains entity mentions which relate to multiple real-world objects or concepts. Such ambiguity poses a threat to the precision and reliability of analyses, thus making linking and disambiguation important steps within NLP systems. In the text processing step, entity linking connects mentions of entities within a given piece of text to actual entities stored in a knowledge base or an ontology. Once these mentions are linked to their canonical entities, analysts can disambiguate ambiguous references and coherently connect

A solution to this problem is applying graph-based techniques, which manage the connections linking entities and their attributes, allowing the system to deduce the correct entity by reasoning over the relationships of the associated entities. Furthermore, the application of entity disambiguation machine learning algorithms within diverse and rich contextual datasets improves the selection of entity candidates for disambiguation with marked improvements in precision and recall. There are still problems of handling ambiguous references, acronyms, and abbreviations — especially in a multi-lingual setting — that as of yet have not been solved. Solving them requires very different approaches using linguistic and extra-linguistic domain specialised knowledge alongside sophisticated computing algorithms. While there is still work to be done in entity linking and disambiguation to improve information extraction, the potential impact of advancements in these areas is tremendous for evolving natural language processing systems, giving intelligence analysts the capability to discern and analyse core information with confidence in its accuracy.

Tools and Technologies: A Survey of NLP Assets for Entity Recognition

In the case of information extraction in the intelligence analysis domain, entity recognition is a vital step that relies on efficient tools and technologies. Proper natural language processing (NLP) has specific tools aimed at meeting these goals. Each of these NLP assets has unique characteristics, functionalities, and constraining factors. A key instrument in entity recognition is the Named Entity Recognition (NER) libraries and APIs which help to automatically extract and classify entities such as persons, organisations, locations, dates and several others from unstructured text data. Analysts are provided with NER tools that can either be accessed through open-source libraries like SpaCy and NLTK or through commercial offerings by other technology giants. Such NER tools are crucial in dealing with huge amounts of text that contain valuable entities. Furthermore, entity recognition is frequently accompanied with in-depth parsing of the syntactic and semantic structures which cannot be carried out without some indispensable tools like dependency parsing and semantic role labeling. These tools do not only help in determining the relationships between the identified entities, but also aid in extracting deep context from the complicated text using advanced machine learning techniques. Recently, advanced machine and deep learning techniques have been developed that utilise large datasets to train particular models for entity recognition which can work accurately and adapt to various domains and languages.

Models such as BERT and GPT, which use transformers, have incorporated contextual data and nuanced entity semantics, thus improving entity recognition. In addition to these core technologies, knowledge bases and ontologies integrated with knowledge graphs improve entity ambiguity and enrich semantic representation. Moreover, graph-based techniques along with knowledge graphs enable holistic entity recognition and information extraction by showing pivotal importance in identifying entities and their relations within broader information networks. As emerging technologies in NLP, neural entity linking and cross-lingual entity recognition will further advance innovation within the field of entity recognition, enhancing multi-linguistic interoperability between cross-datasets, languages, and even diverse documents. Intelligence analysts, focusing on tools and technologies suitable for the requirements and objectives of their specific analytical tasks, need to monitor such technologies closely. With the proper NLP assets for entity recognition, analysts are able to enhance and refine their information extraction processes and, at the same time, unlock precious insights concealed within dense layers of text.

Challenges and Pitfalls: Navigating Ambiguity and Inconsistency

The challenges and pitfalls encountered during entity recognition and information extraction in the context of analysis are particularly pronounced within the realm of intelligence analysis. The difficulty an analyst faces in dealing with ambiguity in unstructured text data is one of the more prominent issues. This kind of ambiguity can arise from several considerations such as language, context, or the way certain words are used in a specific domain. Therefore, the attempt to identify and extract relevant entities from text is very challenging. The problem becomes even more difficult in cases of entities with homonymous and polysemous features. A named entity could refer to different people or places or even organisations depending on the context of its usage. Such resolution of these ambiguities demands sophisticated disambiguation and contextual knowledge algorithms to avoid the misidentification and misclassification of entities. The problem of inconsistency in citations of entities from different sources also introduces new dimensions in information extraction. Alternative names, spellings, or acronyms used to identify an entity create a problem of establishing links and relations among diverse references of the same entity.

Moreover, the unstructured nature of the text, together with the presence of noise, spelling mistakes, shorthand, and informal language, contributes to increasing the difficulty of achieving precision and uniformity in entity recognition. These problems require a capable NLP algorithm that can understand and untangle the many layers of natural language intricacies while also accommodating the peculiarities of varying data sources. The procedures set also need to emphasise validation and verification in order to eliminate false positives and negatives among the identified entities and guarantee the reliability of the information for further analyses and decisions. As much as there are perplexities and unknowns when dealing with ambiguity, inconsistencies, and vague matters, taking decisive action, evolving NLP frameworks, and employing sharpened contextual cues to guide algorithms will enable surpassing these challenges, bolstering the effectiveness of entity recognition within intelligence processes.

Real-World Applications: Case Studies in Intelligence Gathering

Centers for Advanced Defense Studies' use of natural language processing (NLP) techniques modernised information extraction, analysis, and systematisation in the field of gathering intelligence for national security and strategic undertakings. We have the power to understand the concept of technology's impact more deeply in the intelligence world by evaluating a few real-world case studies. For instance, one case study focuses on the NLP aided data-mining and pattern recognition techniques that enabled the mining of data of online conversations that led to the neutralisation of a terrorist plot. Analyses utilising NLP algorithms for entity recognition and sentiment analysis had empowered them to detect exploitative linguistics associated with the phrases uttered in the previous sentence. Similarly, the operational effectiveness of NLP intelligence tasks was further improved by allowing the rapid analysis of text in multiple languages via machine translation capabilities. The proactive monitoring and studying of social media chatter to highlight potential emerging threats to cybersecurity is yet another compelling case study. Threat-eliciting data could be registered and accumulatively ordered using NLP driven information extraction thus enabling rapid response to vulnerabilities that could have translated to large-scale breaches.

Furthermore, the use of topic modelling algorithms was critical in revealing potential threat vectors which, in other circumstances, would have remained concealed within enormous volumes of unstructured data. These and many more other case studies vividly illustrate the role of NLP technologies in intelligence practices and how it supports national interests and responds to multifaceted security challenges. It is obvious that the purpose-driven deployment of NLP technologies in intelligence turns out not to be an academic projection but a pressing requirement of the contemporary intelligence community, providing breakthrough possibilities in information retrieval, analysis, and the production of actionable intelligence.

Integrating Information Extraction Systems: Strategies and Best Practices

Last but not least is how agencies merge information extraction processes into their workflows. This requires particularly careful attention to strategies and best practices designed to ensure smooth functionality and comprehensive outcomes. We aim at giving the more fundamental aspects of the integration procedure so as to enable the concerned intelligence agency to maximise the benefits of the extraction technologies.

1. Define Clear Objectives: It is critical within pre-emptive intelligence analysis to clearly define the system goals centred around actionable intelligence extracts in relation to information extraction systems objectives. Derived goals can include improving information access, information extraction on requisite parameters setting, improving insight generation efficiency vis-à-vis enhanced data, improving extraction processes and time of insight outputs.

2. Compatibility Assessment: Assess the current infrastructure gaps for information extraction systems and their potential capabilities. Assessment of alignment with current systems and technology infrastructure are paramount for integrations.

3. Smooth Data Harvesting and Operations: Automated processes for real-time updating systems, data routing for real-time receipt, processing, ongoing processing, and circulation of sensitive information. Data ingestion ports on various data extraction interactive tools, layers of data processing subsystems interaction, streaming interfaces should smooth data circulation.

4. Configuration and Crafting: These systems demand their core designs to be configured and tailored to meet specific goals if extracted information is to effectively support intelligence analysis, such as recognition of specific entities and extraction of text using relevant domain terminologies.

5. Safety and Lawfulness: Every integration of classified information handling protocols entails formidable safeguarding measures and validity controls. Employ strict governance accesses, encapsulation schemes, and data flow controls.

6. Monitoring and Maintenance: After integration, define processes for continuous oversight and post-integration maintenance to mitigate any emerging concerns. These processes include active optimisation, bug fixing, and scheduled updates to address evolving adaptive threats.

7. Training and Helpdesk Services: Train thoroughly intelligence, with end users, to ensure they can harness the full value from the integrated information extraction systems. Provide post-training helpdesk services to respond to any issues with system use and improve overall adoption.

8. Organisational Structure – Cross Integration: Have an active consideration for the use of information extraction systems with other more advanced analytical systems and tools available within the agency and deployed within the intelligence community. A mixed infrastructure fosters drastic synergistic impact and high return on investment from the information assets.

With the use of the best practices suggested in this document, all intelligence informing agencies are now able to concentrate on providing advanced technologies for natural language processing to enhance its intelligence gathering and analysis thereafter integrating a streamlined information extraction systems with confidence.

Evaluation Metrics: Measuring the Effectiveness of Entity Recognition

It is pivotal to evaluate the accuracy of an entity recognition system for reliability checking in the context of intelligence analysis. Designing appropriate evaluation metrics enables the quantifying of accuracy, precision, recall, and all other relevant metrics which define the effectiveness of these systems. One such assessment metric is precision which in this context is the ratio of correctly identified entities over the total number of entities identified by the system. Similarly, recall measures the performance of the system in capturing all pertinent entities in the dataset provided. Complementing these metrics is the F1 score which recalibrates the result by finding the mean of precision and recall and therefore provides a more holistic assessment. To further enhance understanding towards the limitations of an entity recognition system, examining the impact of false positives and false negatives is equally imperative.

As every discipline has its intricacies, in the case of intelligence analysis, domain-centric evaluation benchmarks should be framed based on primary needs of information extraction in this domain. Constructing qualitative assessments such as determining the influence of missed entities poses on the analysis can help understand how system performance affects practical application.

Moreover, applying validation methods and multiple real-world datasets improves the rigour of evaluation outcomes. Furthermore, defining the baseline performance of the system through comparative evaluation with human-annotated datasets provides valuable insights into the capabilities and limitations of the system.

As a responsive proactive strategy to the dynamics involved in entity recognition, revising the evaluation criteria is necessary. This covers changes in language, dialect, and newly coined names from different cultures or regions. Also, evaluations in other languages are fundamental to the global deployment of entity recognition systems. Apart from that, further research needs to be done on the impact of machine and deep learning approaches on performance to redefine the objectives set for the system.

The lack of a system for comparing and benchmarking entity recognition systems presents an opportunity for further work to be done in establishing comprehensive evaluation frameworks. The domain of entity recognition would benefit from the use of collaborative design from the community because it would provide set guidelines that would enhance clarity as well as advance the methods used.

Additionally, engaging intelligence analysts and subject matter experts to custom-tailor evaluation metrics based on the nuances of intelligence collecting and analysis will help increase the utility and relevance of entity recognition systems in this case.

Conclusion: Future Directions and Innovations in Entity Extraction

As we conclude our study on entity extraction and information extraction within the framework of intelligence analysis, it is crucial to examine possibilities that may shape the future of this domain. Modern developments in natural language processing (NLP) and artificial intelligence continue to open new opportunities pertaining to advancements in techniques of entity extraction. An innovative approach could be through the adoption of sophisticated machine learning systems combined with knowledge databases of specific domains that will make it possible to create more precise and relevant entity recognition systems relative to the context. Also, the adoption of deep learning architectures, like transformer models, could improve entity extraction by recognising complex semantic and contextual relationships within unstructured textual data. Therefore, there are endless opportunities when it comes to visual and auditory inputs which may enrich entity extraction processes as well as aid in a holistic comprehension of diverse data sources. With modern federated learning frameworks, there are new opportunities to fortify the privacy and security of sensitive intelligence contexts through collaborative model training from different data sources.

Furthermore, the ethical concerns of the implications of privacy, bias mitigation, and transparency pertaining to entity extraction will be focusing on future developments. With the increasing need for intelligence in real time, the combination of entity extraction with stream processing and edge computing is going to improve the efficiency and speed at which intelligence analysts are able to extract insights from the data streams. Lastly, the integration with explainable AI entity extraction frameworks will increase trust and allow analysts to validate the outcomes from sophisticated entity recognition systems which will aid them to rationalise and rely on the sophisticated outputs. To summarise, the possibilities of enhancing intelligence analysis through entity extraction are driven by positive technological advances, ethical boundaries, and real-world needs, which means there has to be more active discourse between several fields, and a need for ever-evolving strategies to fully harness Natural Language Processing aimed at redefining the future of intelligence operations.

4

Gauging Intent and Influence

Sentiment Analysis and Opinion Mining

Overview of Sentiment Analysis and Opinion Mining

Sentiment analysis and opinion mining techniques are increasingly becoming essential for contemporary intelligence operations as they employ sophisticated algorithms to provide meaningful intelligence from large volumes of unstructured data. The definition of sentiment analysis revolves around the categorisation, extraction, and interpretation of sentiments within textual data, while opinion mining focuses on identifying the most important and influential opinions and how they shape trends. These two disciplines help to expose the attitudes of the public towards various issues, their emotions, and the most dominant opinions that exist on a given subject matter which is critical for planning and decision making, especially in intelligence agencies. The significance of these disciplines in intelligence operations has accelerated further due to the development of social media and online discussion and debating platforms because users and participants of such forums provide ample opportunities for diverse opinions and sentiments that are relevant for public and geopolitical discourse. Through natural language processing, machine learning, and semantic analysis, analysts are empowered to access the sentiments and opinions hidden in the enormous volumes of text documents and data available, therefore enriching the intelligence-gathering process.

The importance of sentiment analysis and opinion mining encompasses more than just tracking changing trends; it also includes recognising possible security risks and changes in global public opinion regarding important geopolitical matters. Moreover, the dramatically growing importance of sentiment analysis and opinion mining in intelligence operations highlights the ability to uncover delicate changes in public opinion, allowing for advanced strategies and proactive policymaking. Therefore, this emphasises the necessity for intelligence practitioners to possess the appropriate tools and knowledge required to understand the intricacies of contemporary information environments and transform data into useful intelligence, navigating the vast ocean of unstructured data.

Historical Context and Evolution in Intelligence

The historical roots of sentiment analysis in the domain of intelligence began with the evolution of information retrieval and appraisal. Analysts and leaders throughout history have tried to gauge public emotion and perception concerning issues, policies, and public events. Information in ancient civilisations came through couriers and scouts. The ability to perceive the emotion of a crowd was a skill that aided greatly in the governance decision-making process.

Shifts in technology led to more elaborate techniques of public opinion data collection. With the advent of great wars, strategists mastered the art of assessing the "mood" of the masses. Entire nationalistic campaigns became covers for complex programmes. The popularisation of the theory of public opinion made it clear that one cannot disregard the opinion of their own people or those of opposing countries.

The development of technology facilitated the processes of sentiment analysis and opinion mining in the intelligence field. New forms of media such as newspapers, radio, television, and later the internet had their own advantages and disadvantages in terms of monitoring and analysing public sentiment. Intelligence agencies began reaping the benefits of technology and systematically using algorithms to analyse large volumes of textual information, thus refining the processes and paving the way for the application of natural language processing techniques in intelligence work.

As the capabilities of intelligence services evolved and broadened, the processes of sentiment analysis also changed in complexity and scope. Once the world became digitally connected through communication and social networking sites, the methods and spaces through which people expressed and shared their opinions underwent a dramatic change, resulting in immense amounts of unstructured data to be analysed. This required the processes of sentiment analysis and opinion mining to develop to identify trends, detect attempts at manipulation, as well as understand the contextual relevance of the expressions of sentiments and the contextual reasons behind them.

The past-centred framework of sentiment analysis and opinion mining within intelligence highlights the need to carefully interpret and analyse public opinions as a matter of intelligence. It indicates the consistency spanning the range of approaches and techniques used in the field due to the intense need to transform the collective views of people into synthesised actionable intelligence. These foundations of the past, especially in historical contexts, modern-day frameworks of intelligence analysis use sophisticated techniques to make sense of human thoughts and emotions, applying modern-day technologies.

Technological Foundations: Algorithms and Tools

The algorithms and tools facilitate the extraction, classification, and interpretation of sentiments from textual data. Machine learning algorithms, particularly supervised learning techniques like support vector machines (SVM), naive Bayes classifiers, and neural networks, are used for sentiment analysis. These algorithms make predictions based on new text after being trained on labelled datasets. Unsupervised learning techniques such as clustering and topic modelling are also important for defining and categorising sentiments without labels. NLTK, SpaCy, and Gensim NLP libraries offer numerous functions for tokenisation, part-of-speech tagging, syntactic parsing, and semantic analysis that are prerequisites to sentiment analysis, as well as preprocessing the data. Moreover, sentiment lexicons and dictionaries such as AFINN, VADER, and SentiWordNet, which quantify the emotions contained in the text, assign scores to them and therefore provide invaluable support for sentiment analysis.

The impact of deep learning on sentiment analysis is distinct with the use of recurrent neural networks, long short term memory (LSTM) networks, and BERT or GPT transformers. This is because they capture context and dependencies of language. BERT and GPT empower analysts to comprehend expression and perception deeper than previously possible. In turn, enhancing the accuracy and depth of intelligence sentiment analysis. The advancement of technology and development of new algorithms and tools enables the creation of state-of-the-art instruments that innovatively refine the deconstruction and intelligently mine sentiment analysis within the complex wealth of information hidden in textual data.

Sentiment Analysis: Methodologies and Approaches

Sentiment analysis or opinion mining is a systematic process of identifying, extracting, quantifying, and scrutinising text-based information using complex natural language processing techniques. This process seeks to unlock subjectivity from various texts. The aims of this subsection focus on the discourse of multifaceted techniques adopting sentiment analysis and expand the corresponding computational tools and algorithms used to recognise and manipulate the sentiment patterns.

The first step in determining the sentiment of a given text is to leverage a set of resources like lexicons and linguistic rules. Analysts compute the overall sentiment of an entire document by first assigning sentiment scores to individual words based on lexicons which include words and phrases with positive or negative sentiments. This methodology requires constant improvement to incorporation of specialised vocabulary and usage of language in day-to-day life.

Another key methodology includes machine learning, whereby models are trained on labelled datasets to identify and differentiate distinct sentiments. Widely known supervised learning methods, including Support Vector Machines, Decision Trees, and Neural Networks, have

been used to enhance sentiment classification in identification of sentiments proving to be very accurate. Also
important in the discovery of underlying structures and
trends of sentiment in unlabeled data are unsupervised
learning methods such as clustering and latent semantic
analysis.

Along with this, the use of recurrent and convolu-
tional neural networks deep learning models has greatly
improved sentiment analysis by depicting dynamic linguistic elements and contextual details, hence improving
the understanding of complex expressions of sentiment.
Even though these methods are effective, they require
a lot of computing power as well as large datasets to
properly train and validate these models.

Going beyond these principal methods, recent developments in sentiment analysis feature the addition of
multimodal information such as text, images, and video,
and even audio to gain deeper and more accurate insights
into how sentiments are expressed throughout various
media channels. The integration of text with its corresponding images and videos, as well as audio, creates a
new area in sentiment analysis that will bring improved
contextual interpretation and deepen the grasp of sentiments expressed.

In conclusion, understanding the different approaches
and methods in performing a sentiment analysis provides intelligence analysts with powerful capabilities to
identify and interpret the different layers of sentiment

within the textual data index in the constantly growing volume of data. Through the convergence of sophisticated computational capabilities with natural language mastery, analysts can extract valuable insights that form the basis of sentiments and opinions that are dominant in the digital space, enabling strategic stakeholders to handle very complicated decision-making processes with better understanding and prediction.

Detecting Influence Patterns: Case Studies and Examples

Within the scope of intelligence analysis, the capability to detect influence patterns via sentiment analysis and opinion mining is vital in revealing motives and agendas. To this end, we explore impactful case studies and examples that illustrate the real-world consequences and applications of influence pattern detection. Consider, for instance, the study analysing social media communications surrounding the geopolitical event. Sentiment analysis revealed public opinion, which was previously static, shifting in tandem with political developments. This analysis offered critical insights into the prevailing narrative surrounding the event and its implications for political stability in the region. Also, by analysing the language concerning influence in corporate relations, analysts have been able to strategically track influence and anticipate market changes far ahead of their occurrence. Through these examples, it becomes easier to see how sentiment analysis and opinion mining can discern intricate influence patterns in multiple domains and provide intelligence for diverse contexts. Another insightful case includes the use of sentiment analysis for monitoring the circulation of ideological narratives in online forums.

Utilising advanced algorithms, analysts mapped the dissemination of certain sentiments to uncover the major influencers responsible for spreading polarising viewpoints. These findings are invaluable in illuminating societal divisions, predicting potential civil unrest, and designing counter-narratives. In other contexts, sentiment analysis has been crucial in tracking extremist discourse and pinpointing radicalisation indicators in the context of chronic security threats, thereby strengthening warning mechanisms and informing proactive interventions. These research cases highlight the importance of influence pattern detection in sentiment analysis and opinion mining, demonstrating how these methods significantly enhance strategic decision-making and proactive response planning to changing circumstances.

Challenges in Accuracy and Interpretation

The use of sentiment analysis and opinion mining in the domain of intelligence has critical issues such as accuracy and interpretation. Opinion mining has yet to mature into a process operating with adequate accuracy and interpretation, owing to the highly complicated domain of sentiment expression. Understanding and processing contextually dense, connotative, culture-bound text requires advanced natural language processing (NLP) systems that compute the polarity and intensity of sentiment, context's culture, and society. Moreover, the descriptive problem arises from the subjectivity of human expression. Sentiments and opinions are usually influenced by a person's multi-faceted background or experiences. Therefore, accuracy does require constant change, revision, and evolution of algorithms owing to socio-linguistic shifts and subtleties of expression. Furthermore, the interpretation of sentiment and issues goes beyond the straightforward task of framing them, as capturing the geo-political context, historical references, as well as individual motives requires laborious construction. There exists a systematic web of sentiments and opinions that must be untangled in order to distinguish a pattern with its implications. On top of all that, there is the problem that stems from a lack of precision—ambiguity, noise inherent in the text.

Sentiment analysis can be easily thwarted by ambiguities stemming from colloquialisms, slang, sarcasm, or double entendre. Multi-modal content like images, videos, and audio recordings pose additional interpretive challenges due to a lack of textual clues. Moreover, the fusion of sentiment analysis with other frameworks raises issues of data compatibility, particularly with the blending of sentiment-based analytics and structured quantitative analysis, or other qualitative methods. The need for standardisation stems from the challenge to achieve seamless integration while controlling for biases, discrepancies, and conflicts with other analyses. Overall, addressing the gaps of accuracy and interpretation in both sentiment analysis and opinion mining requires the collaborative effort of advanced algorithm design, interdisciplinary synergy, and the refining of the applicability of sentiment insights within the scope of intelligence analysis.

Integration with Other Analytical Frameworks

Within the domain of intelligence synthesis, the combination of sentiment analysis and opinion mining with other frameworks of analysis is of tremendous geo-strategic importance. The integration of sentiment analysis with other frameworks, for example, its application to statistical analysis, machine learning, or network analysis, deepens the understanding intelligence agencies have of the underlying trends and patterns hidden in the mountains of data they process. Such rigorous approaches enable analysts to corroborate findings with multiple sources, fill information gaps, and derive actionable insight more efficiently.

The wide-ranging applicability of sentiment analysis

to other frameworks of analysis is its contribution to improving the process of trend discovery and predictive modelling. With the help of sentiment analysis, the accuracy of predicted social, political, and economic events can be increased significantly. The incorporation of sentiment analysis into predictive models ensures that public perception on issues and shifts in public sentiment are anticipated, therefore enabling better estimation of probable scenarios. In this way, decision makers are better positioned to anticipate and respond to mitigate risk or leverage emerging opportunities.

Moreover, the interplay of sentiment and network analyses creates new opportunities for gathering intelligence and detecting threats. With the use of both sentiment and network analysis, an analyst can determine key influence nodes within social networks, track their interactions, and even trace the diffusion of sentiments and opinions among various demographic groups. This blended framework allows analysts to understand the dynamics of advocacy and manipulation, discover attempts at orchestrated public opinion shaping, and mitigate enabled engineered challenges or threats arising from narratives shaped by deceitful forces.

Integrated with geospatial analysis, sentiment analysis has the potential to reveal gaps in the perception of sentiment globally and regionally. Analysts are now able to conduct spatial analysis of sentiments by placing the results of sentiment analysis over geospatial maps, thus identifying and analysing areas of heightened and depressed sentiments. This integration helps intelligence agencies to better target regional information and sentiment dynamics, thereby improving information dissemination and crisis response operations.

The combination of sentiment analysis and temporal analysis allows for the investigation of public perception over time and marks historical changes in public opinion, as well as forecasting future shifts. Analysts can mitigate emerging challenges by anticipating surges or downturns in sentiment based on historical event data and significant correlating factors, revealing patterns with faster sentiment change through employing temporal sentiment analysis.

Simply put, incorporating opinion mining and sentiment analysis within intelligence layers enhances the scope and complexity of the analysis, increasing the dimensions through which socio-cultural phenomena are observed to include anticipating trends and informing strategies.

Applications in Strategic Decision-Making

Sentiment analysis and opinion mining provide organisations and intelligence agencies with powerful tools within the domain of strategic decision-making. These tools enable the assessment of perception and sentiment of the public regarding specific matters, products, services, and even government policies. Decision-makers can tailor events, trends, or developments to desired sentiments among target audiences using sentiment analysis powered by natural language processing and machine learning.

One important use of sentiment analysis in brand reputation management concerns the strategic decision-making process. Organisations can track social media conversations, customer reviews, and news articles to gather and analyse information on public sentiment toward their brands, gaining invaluable insight. This enables companies to better manage their reputations by resolving issues promptly, identifying critical areas to embrace, and even improving marketing strategies and customer engagement based on positive sentiments.

Moreover, sentiment analysis is very important in guiding product development and market entry strategies. Businesses make decisions concerning new product introductions, new market entry, or refinement of offerings based on an analysis of consumer sentiment towards existing products or potential offerings. Such an approach reduces the risks associated with introducing new products or services and strategically aligning investments.

Within the scope of political and governmental activities, sentiment analysis serves as a crucial tool for identifying public perception of policies, governance, and other relevant concerns. Policymakers can assess public reception for initiatives and reforms by analysing social media conversations, news pieces, and even public debates. This, in turn, enables governments to inform and engage the public, respond to issues of concern, and craft policies that fulfil the expectations of the people.

Further, forecasting and risk evaluation in sentiment analysis for strategic decision-making is equally important. Organisations can project market trends, avert risks, and take advantage of new opportunities by monitoring changes in public perception concerning economic factors, geopolitical affairs, or specific business sectors. In such an unstable public climate, protectiveness, adaptability, and agility in strategic planning can be well managed.

In conclusion, the applications of sentiment analysis in strategic decision-making are boundless and undoubtedly profound. With increasing recognition from organisations and intelligence agencies towards employing sentiment analysis for informed decisions, the incorporation of this technology will transform the approach to strategic decision-making in an integrated and data-driven society.

Ethical and Privacy Considerations in Sentiment Analysis

Due to the large quantities of personal data to be processed, the issues of ethics and privacy in the emerging fields of sentiment analysis and opinion mining are unavoidably important. The ethical issues in sentiment analysis arise from the harm that may be caused by using data regarded as sensitive, such as sentiment data, for privacy-invasive purposes, or for reputation management. There is also an important problem involved with sentiment bias and discrimination that could operate leveraging the underlying algorithms and result in biased sentiment analysis which may ensure disparate impact and discrimination because of race, ethnicity, gender, or socio-economic class. There are also significant privacy issues in the use of sentiment analysis in the contexts of monitoring because this practice may violate people's freedom to express themselves anonymously and within private spaces. There should also be more focused responsibility for the systematic abuse of the sophisticated means of sentiment analysis tools. Instead, there should be clear access to the techniques and methodologies employed in gathering, processing, and analysing the data. Thus, stronger claims can be put forward by the methods of sentiment analysis aimed at privilege analysis where sentiment and emotions are addressed within analytical frameworks.

An ethical issue relates to analysing data, acquiring informed consent from users whose data is being used – especially when sentiment analysis applies to social media or other public domains. Protecting the rights and privacy of individuals while recognising the significant advantages attained from sentiment analysis requires serious contemplation and ethical supervision. Analysts and organisations also have an obligation to maintain strict data governance, privacy, and security protocols to defend against misuses of sentiment analysis in order to comply with ethics norms of intelligence and analytics. With ongoing advancements in the field of sentiment analysis, greater emphasis must be placed on establishing proactive ethics policies and respecting privacy regulations.

Future Directions: Innovations and Emerging Trends

With the continuous advances in Natural Language Processing (NLP), there are a number of new and exciting innovations which are developing trends at the intersection of sentiment analysis, opinion mining, and intelligence analysis. One of the more pronounced developments to watch is the use of sophisticated algorithms like deep learning and neural networks for more precise and granular sentiment analysis. These technologies have been found helpful in capturing subtle contextual cues and nuances in unstructured text and, thus, help enhance the accuracy of sentiment classification and opinion extraction. Furthermore, the emergence of multimodal sentiment analysis that goes beyond text to visually and audibly analyse speech is a transformative development that could greatly enhance the ability to capture sentiment across different channels of communication. This comprehensive approach opens new horizons toward a more profound understanding of human expression and sentiment intelligence. There also seems to be an infinite capacity for exploring the influence, persuasion, and social interaction within large, complex systems of communication brought about by the coupling of sentiment analysis to network analysis and graph theory.

Analysing the relationship between sentiment clusters and information diffusion enables analysts to understand the critical factors that influence the mechanisms of influence and opinion dissemination. This understanding results in better decision-making. In addition, the evolving xAI as well as the interpretable ML models have been addressing the transparency and accountability gaps in the sentiment analysis systems used in intelligence contexts where the need for information sensitivity is paramount. With these models, analysts can explain the reasons for making sentiment predictions and identify crucial determinants that drive specific sentiments which in turn supports trust in the analytic products. At the same time, these developments are being complemented by interdisciplinary work from psychology and linguistics on the computing side aimed at creating sentiment analysis systems which take into account thinking, culture, and language. This approach goes beyond cultures and languages and aims at providing a more comprehensive understanding of sentiments from diverse populations and geopolitical contexts. To sum up, the sentiments and opinion mining with other emerging trends is shaped by the integration of advanced technologies, emerging directions of innovative inter-disciplinary research with the responsible, ethical...

By adopting these changes, intelligence agencies will be able to leverage sentiments of the vast unstructured data to acquire the most important insights, improving their ability to manoeuvre through intricate geopolitics.

5

Uncovering Hidden Narratives

Topic Modelling and Document Clustering

Introduction to Hidden Narratives in Intelligence

The strategic application of natural language processing (NLP) technologies in intelligence analysis reveals hidden narratives which could provide strategic insights and a significant intelligence advantage. Analysts can interpret multilayered scenarios and untangle complex interrelationships, identifying crucial patterns that are often overlooked by conventional analysis techniques. Patterns that are not immediately visible but are essential for shaping key decisions, uncovering potential risks, and revealing proactive opportunities are often referred to as hidden narratives. When narratives are harnessed effectively, intelligence professionals can anticipate developments and preemptively respond with greater precision and foresight.

With regard to more nuanced issues, hidden narratives shed light on relationships interlinking diverse factors, revealing the "how" and "why" of deeper contextual frameworks. The capacity to provide this additional context greatly enhances the identification of latent trends, micro-level indicators, or even obfuscated signals that may pose serious implications for national security, geopolitical tensions, or corporate risk management. Analysts equipped with skills necessary to explore these concealed narratives earn the power to construct sound assessments, accurate forecasts, and devise plans that suit the primary goals. In other words, the powerful ability to unravel concealed narratives using advanced NLP algorithms can transform intelligence practices and strategies by expanding the operational and analytical efficiency.

Furthermore, the uncovering of concealed stories through sophisticated NLP methods fosters a more advanced response to shifting threats, allowing for preemptive measures to be taken based on trends. By identifying indicators of potential threats or emerging opportunities, intelligence analysts can neutralise opposing strategies, manage risks, and take advantage of beneficial circumstances. This proactive attitude supports enhanced agility, resilience, preparedness, and the ability to anticipate evolving and uncertain security environments.

In conclusion, the advanced pursuit of hidden narratives through NLP to extract intelligence and actionable insights reflects a more advanced method of knowledge acquisition and exploitation. It makes it possible to obtain actionable intelligence from a wide and varied range of information by turning raw data into useful information that is processed and analysed. With this information, organisations can improve their spending, develop better operational plans, and protect their principal interests. This pursuit marks a fundamental advancement in intelligence analysis. Adopting this approach enables stakeholders to better understand and respond to the complex web of global interactions and new developments.

Conceptual Framework: Topic Modelling and its Relevance

In the realm of intelligence analysis, topic modelling is one of the most important methodologies as it helps reveal the hidden structures and spatial-temporal patterns contained in massive amounts of unstructured data. Like many tools, it originated in natural language processing (NLP). Topic modelling provides a methodology for finding, recognising, and extracting recurring themes/tags/subjects from texts. Properly set recurring themes can help reveal invaluable narratives so that analysts understand the real content and perceptions behind the documents.

The importance of intelligence topic keyboards is more than obvious. Information is growing exponentially with new datasets, putting an insurmountable amount of data on organisations and making it more difficult to discover meaningful trends, relationships, and recurring events. In this sense, topic modelling helps to navigate the tumultuous ocean of data by simplifying its structure into easily digestible themes and topics. Also, while dealing cross-lingually with heterogeneous multilingual datasets, it is highly useful because of its ability to overcome language barriers and capture the underlying concepts.

To grasp the broad principles of topic modelling, one must explore the mathematics and statistics involved in the extraction of latent topics. A well-known algorithm in this area is Latent Dirichlet Allocation (LDA), which employs probabilistic models for word and document-to-topic distribution mappings. Beyond LDA, there are several other more LDA approaches such as Non-negative Matrix Factorisation (NMF) and Latent Semantic Analysis (LSA) which further strive to uncover the semantic structures within textual data.

Beyond having applications in pattern detection, the importance of topic modelling goes far beyond this; it is important for informed decision making and anticipatory intelligence. Analysts can identify, monitor, and anticipate dynamic trend evolution, social movements, as well as geopolitical changes and inform decision makers and other stakeholders regarding the emerging unfolding narratives. Furthermore, the combination of topic modelling with other NLP tools such as sentiment analysis and entity recognition enhances the precision and depth of intelligence interpretation, transforming them into interpret and act upon.

Understanding the importance of the conceptual framework of topic modelling vis-à-vis unlocking the true value of unstructured data in intelligence analysis. Within this area and assessing its value, the information and decision-makers will be able to draw a coherent story from the information tapestry thereby improving their ability to understand, predict and act on complex events and phenomena.

Key Algorithms: Latent Dirichlet Allocation and Beyond

One of the key algorithms in the field of topic modelling is Latent Dirichlet Allocation (LDA), which is fundamental to exposing underlying themes in vast textual datasets. This algorithm is based on the idea that each document in a given corpus consists of a mixture of topics and each topic is a distribution of words. Using graphical models of probability, LDA seeks to identify the latent topics that exist in a collection of documents and, at the same time, provide a distribution of words over the topics so identified.

The use of topic modelling has evolved with advancements like the Hierarchical Dirichlet Process (HDP) which automatically figures out the number of topics within the data set, making it more flexible. Type, Non-negative Matrix Factorisation or NMF, is known for document clustering and topic extraction, therefore gaining popularity despite not being probabilistic like LDA. More so, the incorporation of time and change in elements as seen in the Dynamic Topic Model, and LDA-M further develop topic modelling.

Mastering such core concepts starts with understanding their algorithms, which are of dire importance along with mathematics around them. Moreover, designers of algorithms must also consider issues such as hyperparameter precision along with the rigidity of the algorithms with diverse textual data. When implementing these algorithms within the context of intelligence analysis, one must derive and interpret the information, while ensuring coherence among themes which needed to be carefully managed.

In the sphere of intelligence, the adoption of Latent Dirichlet Allocation and its more contemporary extensions is essential for gaining holistic and comprehensive insights from unstructured text data. Understanding the strengths and weaknesses of these algorithms is fundamental to harnessing their capabilities in revealing hidden narratives and aiding well-informed decision-making. Analysts tasked with sourcing actionable intelligence from large volumes of text must keep pace with advancements in Natural Language Processing (NLP) and novel approaches to topic modelling as the discipline matures.

Data Preparation: Preprocessing Techniques and Challenges

In the context of intelligence analysis, the application of document clustering and topic modelling starts with a pivotal step: data refinement. This step entails the cleansing, reshaping, and formatting of nascent raw data into an analysable structure. In the sphere of natural language processing (NLP), the emphasis placed on preprocessing techniques stems from the unstructured characteristic of text data. The overarching aim of data refinement is to uphold the quality of input data, curtail noise, and harmonise the text for subsequent advanced analysis.

Text normalisation is one of the most important preprocessing steps. This includes processes, such as tokenisation, stemming, and lemmatisation, which aim to modify words into their base forms by reducing inflectional forms to the lowest applicable word. Moreover, filtering commonly occurring words that add little value to the analysis, which reduces algorithmic noise to the entire input, is done through stop word removal.

Another important part of text data preparation is dealing with punctuation marks, special characters, and numbers. These character sets need to be removed as they have no value in relation to the text and only act as a hindrance while topic modelling or document clustering. Some intelligence documents may also require the use of encoding methods like UTF-8 to support various languages and character sets.

An additional issue is the presence of multi-lingual datasets; ensuring equivalence in preprocessing steps, as well as domain-specific jargon and acronym deviation, is a challenge. Within the scope of intelligence analysis, the need to protect and preserve privacy may require sensitive data to go through additional steps of anonymisation or de-identification which ensures confidentiality.

It should be understood that preparing data is a process done in cycles because decisions regarding the clean-up of the data should be aligned with the goals of the analysis at hand. While automated systems can aid in streamlining the tasks of data cleaning and validation, human oversight on the automated tools is pivotal concerning the relevance of the data that has been summarised.

In conclusion, the data cleaning process for topic modelling and document clustering within the context of intelligence analysis requires balancing the methodology and the unstructured text to be processed. The approaches and problems experienced during the data cleaning process will significantly impact the quality and usefulness of the results with regard to analysis that follow.

Implementation Strategies: Tools, Platforms, and Techniques

The application of document clustering and topic modelling in the field of intelligence should be accompanied with a thorough appreciation of the frameworks, tools, and platforms that were designed for that purpose.

The remainder of this chapter provides the analysts with the necessary insight and techniques to put these sophisticated approaches to practice.

Tools are the key to implementing any strategy. In the case of NLP, there is a wide range of tools, each with its specific characteristics. From open-source libraries such as NLTK and spaCy to commercial ones like IBM Watson or Google Cloud's Natural Language API, all of them require a thorough evaluation of their strengths and weaknesses for optimal selection with respect to the needs of any particular NLP tasks.

Furthermore, the selection of a specific platform is equally important to ensure proper completion of the task at hand. Whether it is an on-premises solution or a cloud-based one, factors such as scalability, security, and integration need to be evaluated against organisational requirements, making the selection appropriate. Moreover, with AI and NLP advancing rapidly, emerging platforms will need to be monitored closely in order to remain at the frontier.

For document vision involving topic or cluster modelling, the implementation techniques are more complex. Some of the basic components are text data preprocessing, feature extraction, and model selection. Analysts need to know how to clean raw data and arrange it into a structured format, which requires processes like tokenisation, lemmatisation, and filling empty fields. Moreover, making use of striving methods such as TF-IDF, word embeddings, and document-term matrices will improve model performance, hence having expertise in feature extraction is crucial.

Strategy implementation goes further beyond the techniques employed to encompass organisational structures as well. Organisational collaboration is facilitated through the use of collaborative tools as well as version control systems which help in team NLP project participation. In addition to that, the creation of these documents provides a means through which operational model deployment is automated within intelligence processes, model deployment while ensuring uniformity is achieved within different processes across operations.

Recapitulating the above points, one understands that in the context of intelligence operations, the application of topic modelling and document clustering tools requires robust implementation strategies focusing on platforms, analytics, and document processing tools. Moreover, thorough studies of these intelligence tools enable an analyst to develop means of revealing complex datasets, patterns, make significant data-driven decisions, and tell compelling stories backed by evidence and useful intelligence.

Case Studies: Successful Applications in Intelligence

Natural language processing (NLP) methods have brought forth profound advancements in virtually every intelligence domain. Through extensive case studies, we will explore how NLP techniques have been applied to text documents, revealing stories that were previously buried within layers of text and providing intelligence that was deeply actionable. One example is the assessment of openly available data concerning international relations and possible conflict and security issues. Topic modelling was instrumental in allowing analysts to discover new themes and patterns in free-form text, thus facilitating proactive risk assessment and greater strategic foresight. Also, in counter-terrorism, document clustering techniques consolidated diverse and dispersed resources, which included informal internet fora, social media channels, and phone calls and texts from suspected terrorists, yielding vital insights into evolving techniques, telematic networks, and looming dangers. Perhaps one of the most fascinating case studies demonstrates the use of sentiment analysis to track public emotions and forecast civil unrest in acute conflict zones. NLP algorithms enabled the shift in public sentiments to be detected and, together with other indicators, the potential risk for political strife assessed, thus allowing timely actions and targeted preemptive response.

Moreover, NLP was critical to the financial intelligence division in fraud detection through the scrutiny of massive volumes of text data like communiqués, transactions, and regulatory documents. The use of named entity recognition NLP methods aided in identifying people or organisations and their complex relationships which helped in making major progress towards revealing hidden financial crimes and even money laundering. In all these instances, the effectiveness of NLP applied to intelligence demonstrates, on the one hand, multifaceted its use, and on the other hand highlights the need to sharpen analytical and situational intelligence tools for the benefit of the intelligence community. These examples underscore how much NLP enriches the intelligence domain by exposing the intelligence gaps and requirements while eliminating the risks, thus enabling more calculated decisions.

Document Clustering: Methodologies and Approaches

Intelligence analysis document clustering is an essential part of natural language processing (NLP), and it enables the grouping of similar documents together. This part discusses the strategies and techniques systematised towards effective document clustering in intelligence. First, it has to be noted that document clustering is an unsupervised learning problem, which means that the algorithm tries to discern patterns and structures within the unlabelled data set. One of the basic principles underlying document clustering is the application of vector space models through which documents are treated as vectors in a high dimensional space, thus making similarity calculations possible. Moreover, some hierarchical clustering methods like agglomerative and divisive clustering are important in classifying documents into meaningful clusters, which help the analysts in discovering trends and insights that are often hidden. Besides, more complex and heterogeneous intelligence datasets are often approached with more robustness through density-based clustering of varying shapes and sizes like DBSCAN. Along with these methodologies, now add the graph-based clustering methods which form cohesive clusters using the relationships between documents further exposing interconnected themes and topics that provide useful insights.

With the advancement of NLP, deep learning methods, especially those using neural network-based clustering techniques, are increasingly popular because they can automatically extract features and learn complex patterns within the data. In intelligence analysis, the selection of a suitable clustering method is based on the type of dataset, the purpose of the analysis, and how interpretable the formed clusters should be. Exploring different clustering methods for the intelligence data improves the efficiency of the analysts' workflows. Ultimately, intelligence analysts are able to sift through vast amounts of unstructured text data and turn them into valuable insights that strengthen strategic decision-making after mastering various clustering techniques and understanding their applications.

Evaluating Effectiveness: Metrics and Performance Measures

Evaluating the effectiveness of topic modelling and document clustering in the context of intelligence analysis requires assessing how accurate and reliable the insights that stem from these NLP techniques are. Achieving this goal relies on selecting appropriate metrics and performance measures. Topic coherence is one of the most crucial metrics in evaluating the performance of a topic model. Coherence measures the interpretability of topics as symbols within a given circle of words with a degree of relationship. More meaningful topics, which are crucial for revealing concealed narratives within voluminous unorganised data, lead to higher scores in coherence. There are also additional measures known as perplexity and convergence time which aim to measure the quality and efficiency of topic models. These help analysts to judge the models' forecasting power and computational efficiency for further assessment. When dealing with document clustering, computational methods using purity, entropy, or silhouette score seem to yield the best results. Purity benchmarks the cluster's homogeneity to ensure that each group predominantly consists of documents from a single category or topic.

Entropy, in this case, helps in quantifying the degree of disorder in the assignment of documents to clusters. It also provides a measure of the distribution and diversity of the documents within clusters. While assessing the overall performance of the clustering algorithm, one must evaluate cluster compactness and separation using the silhouette score. Further, the evaluation process needs to be customised for intelligence analysis, tailored to its context, which calls for domain-specific metrics. For example, in security and threat evaluation, metrics concentrating on outlier and anomaly detection with NLP tend to assess the efficacy of techniques profoundly. More importantly, the evaluation of NLP techniques in intelligence analysis is fundamentally not limited to quantitative dimensions; it includes qualitative dimensions rendered by specialists in the subject matter. This comprises manually scrutinising the topics and documents that have been clustered to ascertain that the output is meaningful and relevant. Additionally, the strength of the evaluation is anchored on the use of different NLP techniques to refine the assessment for hidden narratives, thereby utilising multiple performance metrics to evaluate, in juxtaposition, the techniques' collective performance.

Continued research and development of novel evaluation metrics will enrich the process of gauging the effectiveness of topic modelling and document clustering in NLP with particular regard to intelligence analysis.

Integrative Analysis: Combining Results with Other NLP Techniques

Integrative analysis refers to the synthesis of all results from various techniques in a particular order which, in more advanced cases, can be used for better extraction of intelligence from a given piece of information. The described approach serves as an illustration of a paramount strategy for enhancing the usefulness and value of the analytical products and, therefore, strengthens the advantages of technology offered to intelligence analysts in the course of making decisions backed by an understanding of the information domain. Here, we analyse integrative analysis, focusing on its significance, frameworks, and implications in the context of intelligence.

The merging of results from different NLP techniques, including entity recognition, sentiment analysis, topic modelling, and document clustering, is called integration analysis. It has been observed that combining the results from all methods increases the ability to unravel intricate relationships, emergent patterns, and hidden narratives which would remain unexplored if each technique was applied separately. Such thorough analysis enhances the validity of the findings as well as understanding of the matter.

As mentioned before, diverse NLP techniques need to

be organised in some manner to allow integration analysis to flow properly; thus, a solid structure is necessary to synchronise outputs. It is important that these results are organised to allow sophisticated analysis as well as holistic interpretation. Furthermore, using visual mappings or other interactive systems can provide the needed frameworks and allow complex integrated outputs to be conveyed and explored for refined insights.

Additionally, integrative analysis encourages a more holistic view that goes beyond the use of one NLP technique. This method takes advantage of the combined or collective strengths of different approaches, which in turn allows analysts to address more difficult problems with a greater arsenal, thus increasing the ability to mitigate the effects of biases, mistakes, or failures that are bound to happen when using a singular approach.

To sum up, the integrative analysis is one of the most critical approaches to strengthening the application of NLP in intelligence work. An intelligence analyst can synthesise the results of different NLP techniques, elucidating complex relationships, extracting important insights, and generating sophisticated assessments that inform strategic action. The importance of integrative analysis for deriving meaningful intelligence from disparate outputs produced by different NLP techniques will only continue to grow alongside advancements in technology and increasing complexity of textual data.

Future Directions: Advancements and Opportunities in Topic Modelling

It is indisputable that topic modelling has transformed natural language processing (NLP) within the realm of intelligence analysis. In carving out new avenues for innovation, emerging technologies and challenges simultaneously pose new hurdles. One critical advancement for the future of topic modelling lies within the scope of improving its algorithms scalability and efficiency. There is an ever-growing need for effective models that can process datasets accurately, both in volume and complexity.

The implementation of deep learning algorithms within advanced topic modelling presents an area for enhanced capabilities. With the use of neural networks, every researcher and analyst would be able to pursue more sophisticated relationships between the texts, thus obtaining better insights into the intertwined narratives. Moreover, real-time data streams integrated with topic modelling pose an exciting new challenge. The capacity to alter and adapt topic models in real time as data inputs change could improve the speed and relevance of insights generated from intelligence data. Lastly and perhaps most importantly, the consequences of topic modelling in relation to ethics and intelligence require further examination.

With the utmost attention to privacy, bias, and fairness, how models are approached and applied within a given field is bound to carve out new dimensions of interest given its growth. The regulation of topic modelling techniques will be rooted in ethical frameworks which are likely still under development. It is undoubtedly promising to think of blending topic modelling with other modalities like audio-visual data. Topic modelling frameworks are capable of multimedia content analysis by utilising diverse image, video, and audio data, thereby enabling analysts to extract deeper insights from intelligence datasets. The interrelation of topic modelling together with knowledge graphs and ontologies offers a significant advantage. Analysts are able to use semantic relationships and structured knowledge representations to retrieve and analyse complex contextual information which offers a more rounded perspective of intelligence data. To wrap up, intelligence analysis holds immense prospects when blended together with topic modelling. We expect stronger capabilities in the coming generations of topic modelling, thanks to the deep learning integration, real-time adaptability, ethics, multimodal fusion, scalable frameworks, and knowledge graph convergence. This, in turn, will create even more refined and influential intelligence insights.

6

Breaking Down Barriers

Machine Translation and Cross-Lingual NLP

Introduction to Machine Translation and Cross-Lingual NLP

Machine translation is a crucial part of cross-lingual natural language processing (NLP) that has changed the way people and organisations communicate and access information in multiple languages. We will examine the foundations of machine translation and its role in breaking down language barriers to promote global integration.

The development of machine translation, from traditional rule-based approaches to the advent of neural machine translation (NMT) models, represents an ongoing quest for accuracy and fluency in cross-linguistic communication. To understand why machine translation is important for effective cross-lingual communication, one must first appreciate the intricacies of different languages as well as dialects, which are laden with cultural subtleties. Furthermore, globalisation has intermingled diverse linguistic communities requiring more seamless translations that are accurate too. Additionally, the increasing significance of machine translation in facilitating efficient knowledge transfer, business transactions, and diplomatic engagements across language borders underscores its indispensability in today's interconnected world. Appreciating that machine translation can transform not only cross-lingual communication but also cooperation and understanding between individuals or institutions all over the globe.

In this examination of machine translation and cross-lingual NLP, we will look at the basics of these technologies, explaining how they help to overcome language barriers and promote a peaceful world conversation.

The Evolution of Machine Translation: From Rule-Based to Neural Approaches

Machine translation has undergone an astonishing metamorphosis from the traditional rule-based approaches to modern neural network models, signifying a fundamental change in how cross-lingual communication is achieved. The initial rule-based systems that depended on linguistic rules and dictionaries were limited in their ability to capture the subtleties and intricacies of natural language thereby often causing translations that lacked fluency and accuracy. These systems needed labour-intensive manual coding of grammatical rules and syntactic structures for each pair of languages, which made scalability and adaptability difficult. However, statistical machine translation (SMT) emerged with improvements in computational linguistics and artificial intelligence. SMT models used large bilingual corpora to deduce the best possible translation by using probability and statistics for improved accuracy. This was a major improvement over rule-based systems as it enabled translating more text with better fluency and coherence. Despite being a step forward, SMT still had difficulty dealing with peculiarities or ambiguities found in real languages. This ushered in the era of neural machine translation (NMT), driven by deep learning algorithms and parallel computing.

Machine translation was revolutionised by NMT models, which directly map input sentences to output translations without the need for intermediate representation or complex feature engineering. The advent of attention mechanisms has also improved the ability of NMT models to capture long-range dependencies and contextual information, thereby resulting in more contextually appropriate and fluent translations. Neural models have also outperformed previous approaches in dealing with morphologically rich languages and low-resource languages, thus overcoming one of the main limitations of previous approaches. The development of machine translation continues with current transformer-based architectures like BERT series and GPT series that are well known for improving contextual semantics understanding as well as global coherence in translations. These improvements have resulted in machine translation reaching unprecedented levels of accuracy and fluency, making it a vital tool for global communication, cross-border collaborations, multilingual knowledge dissemination etc.

Core Technologies in Cross-Lingual Understanding: An Overview

Once we begin to look into cross-lingual understanding, it becomes crucial to examine the core technologies that underpin this area. The groundwork for successful cross-lingual understanding is laid by having robust and adaptive language processing mechanisms. One such technology is bilingual lexicons, which are repositories of bilingual word pairs that facilitate mapping between words in different languages. Furthermore, statistical machine translation (SMT) is essential in analysing parallel corpora to obtain translations by using probabilistic models to select the most appropriate linguistic equivalences. A game-changer in cross-lingual understanding has been neural machine translation (NMT), which uses neural networks to produce more contextually accurate translations by considering entire sentences rather than fragments. Cross-lingual word embeddings also assist in aligning semantically similar words across languages thereby enhancing efficient cross-lingual information retrieval and analysis. Another important technology is multilingual named entity recognition which helps identify and categorise entities in multilingual content thus supporting cross-lingual knowledge extraction and analysis. Multilingual topic modelling techniques help reveal shared themes among various languages enabling a more profound comprehension of cross-lingual textual data.

Cross-lingual sentiment analysis tools are very important for understanding emotions and opinions in different languages, which is important for understanding subtle cross-lingual communication. Lastly, cross-lingual summarisation algorithms make it possible to condense multilingual texts while retaining crucial information. This makes it easier to understand and analyse cross-lingual content. This broad overview highlights the importance of these key technologies in enabling effective cross-lingual comprehension, and underscores their central role in bridging linguistic gaps that enhance intelligence decision making.

Application in Intelligence: Bridging Language Gaps for Enhanced Decision-Making

In the intelligence field, it is important to bridge language gaps in order to make effective decisions. This is facilitated by machine translation and cross-lingual NLP technologies that allow analysts and agencies to access, analyse, and understand information from different languages. These advanced systems enable intelligence professionals to get valuable insights from foreign language content by converting text and speech between languages seamlessly thereby expanding actionable intelligence. Through machine translation and cross-lingual NLP applications, global communications can be efficiently monitored by intelligence organisations, intercepted messages decrypted and a complete picture of foreign perspectives developed hence improving their situational awareness as well as strategic response capabilities. Moreover, these technologies help identify emerging threats in real time, promote cross-border collaboration and assist in diplomatic processes through efficient communication across language barriers. Furthermore, when dealing with multilingual societies or international operations; the integration of machine translation and cross-lingual NLP increases the ability of intelligence agencies to interact with different communities thus enhancing community relations and trust building.

Additionally, the use of these tools enhances resource management and reduces dependence on human translators, thus simplifying operations and increasing productivity. As organisations grapple with a complex global security environment, the strategic employment of machine translation and cross-lingual NLP is critical for overcoming language barriers and exploiting untapped information sources. The convergence of these technologies with intelligence activities marks a new age in improved decision-making, strategic foresight and proactive risk management that places agencies at the forefront in addressing emerging threats in a multilingual world.

Handling Low-Resource Languages: Challenges and Innovations

Machine translation and cross-lingual natural language processing (NLP) have unique challenges when it comes to low-resource languages. These are languages that do not have enough digital resources such as training data, parallel corpora, or linguistic annotations. Consequently, creating effective translation models for low-resource languages is a difficult task that requires innovative approaches and careful consideration of different factors. The first challenge in dealing with low-resource languages is the lack of written texts and spoken data in these languages. This dearth makes it hard to train robust machine translation models since algorithms depend on large amounts of high-quality data for learning and optimisation purposes. Moreover, low-resource languages often display morphological complexity, dialectal variations as well as lack standardised orthographies which make them more complex for NLP systems. To overcome these challenges, researchers and practitioners in this field have been exploring novel methods while also leveraging advances in transfer learning and unsupervised learning techniques. These methods are aimed at transferring knowledge from resource-rich to low-resource languages thus addressing the problem of sparse data. Additionally, initiatives focusing on community-driven data collection and collaboration with native speakers have emerged to create more comprehensive and representative datasets for low-resource languages.

Moreover, the researchers are studying how to combine linguistic typology and typologically-informed models in order to better capture the structural and typological properties of low-resource languages for effective machine translation and cross-lingual NLP. Another important aspect of addressing low-resource languages is creating robust evaluation metrics that take into account their unique characteristics and challenges. Traditional evaluation metrics may not accurately reflect the performance of machine translation systems for low-resource languages; hence there is a need for customised evaluation frameworks. Also, dynamic adaptation as well as domain adaptation techniques design and implementation are key in optimising translation systems for low-resource languages, enabling them to be more adaptable and relevant across different contexts. The research on handling low-resource languages is an ongoing process that has the potential to significantly impact linguistic diversity preservation, communication accessibility, and global information exchange.

Integration with Existing Systems: Seamless Multilingual Communication

As businesses expand and operate globally, smooth multilingual communication has become essential for collaboration. In intelligence and security, the need for accurate interpretation and analysis of information from various sources amplifies this need. This is especially true for the integration with existing systems, which helps agencies consolidate and disseminate intelligence cross-linguistically. Here, the focus is on the integration of machine translation and cross-lingual NLP technologies with frameworks and workflows to enable seamless multilingual communication. With the aid of these technologies, intelligence agencies are better able to preserve information during translation processes and use decisions based on analysis from different languages.

Other key integration issues include legacy systems, analytic tools, secure data transfer protocols, and system boundaries in user experience framework. Meeting these requirements helps ensure that the system works with analyst and operative workflows and preferences. Furthermore, the integrated solutions must be flexible and robust to address rapidly evolving multilingual intelligence contexts.

Seamless multilingual communication requires preserving the intricacies of a document's context, cultural references, and meaning throughout the translation and analysis processes. Domain contextualisation is essential to enhancing the understanding of specific fields that forward accuracy and eloquence in the translation models used, thus improving the rendition of the source material.

Implementing cross-lingual machine translation and integrating cross-lingual and multilingual natural language processing technologies into existing frameworks demands rigorous quality assurance processes to determine the dependability of the translated texts. This combines quantitative techniques of translation validation employing BLEU and METEOR metrics, which require human judgement for capturing qualitative and intricate linguistic intricacies and ambiguities. Rigorous integration of cross-lingual NLP technologies, coupled with precise quality control assessment frameworks, establishes an infrastructure for streamlined, multilingual communications that underpin actionable intel gleaned from diverse linguistic matrices and myriad texts by intelligence agencies.

The goals for seamless multilingual communication within the scope of intelligence and security have now been technologically aided by advancements in machine translation and cross-lingual NLP, proving its successful implementation along with systems sophistication.

Successfully overcoming the challenges of this process allows agencies to use language in a way that goes beyond simple communication, enabling them to obtain valuable intelligence from a variety of sources.

Evaluating Accuracy and Reliability: Metrics in Machine Translation Quality Assessment

Each machine translation system should be evaluated against the criteria of making certain systems highly precise and reliable. Making automated translations involves a lot of checking in order to determine how accurate the automated translations are. With different systems and different metrics associated with machine translations, automatic translations get simpler every time. In all centralised automatic translation systems, some measured criteria can be used to establish the efficiency of a machine translation system. One important measure in automation translation is BLEU where a certain translation is evaluated against other provided reference translations. Equally performed NIST evaluations scan translations for comprehension and smoothness by comparing them against human translations to cross-check how well they estimate the original document. All of these metrics produce a translation and give a unique way of estimating the empowerment of any machine translation system. Evaluations of machine translations go beyond metrics. Quantised translating is done primarily with metrics, but the overall effectiveness of the machine translation still predominantly depends on a person's evaluation of the text's context, accuracy, checking over its translation grammar, integrity, and holistic semantics. In this case, the automated translation is evaluated subjectively over basic principles to deliver value-added domains which usually machine translation methods do not take into account.

Evaluating translations requires stakeholders to take domain-specific details and language subtleties into account, ensuring the product meets context and purpose requirements with respect to the intelligence analysis. With the development of new technologies, there are new evaluation methods, such as metrics based on modern neural models, which use deep learning structures to assess a text's translation quality in terms of its similarity and coherence considering the context. While these new evaluation metrics become more advanced, machine translation still requires further development, making these new models more sophisticated. Further, with each refinement of the models, there is a new challenge or opportunity that needs to be addressed, which in turn requires reevaluating and reinventing the solutions. Evaluating the precision and credibility of machine translation is the outcome of technological evolution on demand along with the growing need for multilingual intelligence analysis. By employing various traditional and modern metrics, translators and stakeholders will have greater confidence in decisions evaluated based on machine translation systems employed within the intelligence domain.

Overcoming Contextual Ambiguities: Context-Aware Translation Techniques

The importance of context when translating terms cannot be overstated, especially in the case of phrases that rely on surrounding text for meaning. We need to analyse the problems posed by contextual ambiguities in cross-lingual NLP and the methods that have been developed to resolve them.

With different cultural and linguistic contexts, the same word can be interpreted in various ways, making the translation process very puzzling. This poses a significant problem for machine translation systems. The machine learning paradigm aims to address this challenge by drawing from the overarching environment within which the words are situated. In one such attempt, sophisticated algorithms are employed to scan the text that surrounds the phrase intending to access contextual markers that would facilitate accurate translation.

Moreover, the understanding of context in translations can be enhanced when relevant background information is added, as in legal or technical texts where some terms have meanings beyond their everyday use. Translation models that account for context use specialised and main corpora catering to the particular field, which assists them in accurately detecting and translating such texts.

Additionally, the advancement of machine learning and natural language processing has facilitated the application of neural methodologies for context-aware translation. With neural models, complex forms of contextual information from the source language can be captured and encoded, allowing for more precise translations in the target language. This capability enables the systems to capture implicit relationships and perform disambiguation based on contextual linguistics.

Anthropological aspects of culture, including norms, values, and prescriptive models, also present contextual ambiguity in translation. Traditional systems tend to struggle with translating idioms, metaphors, and culturally specific references. Context-aware translations of such texts involve cultural study and cultural adaptation; the aim is to preserve the intended meaning while adjusting to cultural differences.

The importance of real-time adaptation is particularly significant in cross-lingual communication. Contextually aware systems equipped with contextual sensing capabilities can translate a text in real-time while adjusting the translation to the discussion as it evolves, maintaining cohesive cross-lingual discourse.

In summary, contextual ambiguity in translation can be addressed from different perspectives, including linguistic domain analysis, domain expertise, culture, computation, technology, and context-aware translation techniques. Such methods improve the precision and fluency of multi-language communication and accelerate collaboration and understanding between speakers of different languages.

Operational Protocols: Deploying Secure and Scalable Translation Solutions

Strategies that translate intelligence into actionable cross-lingual NLP systems necessitate a focus on confidentiality in global intelligence agencies. The operational policies relevant here in information technology are sophisticated and resilient to adaptive scrutiny. There are many trade factors adhering to data assurance and solution infrastructure.

Advanced layered solution architecture informs several axial cases which are driven towards achieving seamless orchestration process workflows. At Command & Control, securing information while granting access to other functions enhances system intelligence. Command categories obtain precise outputs with dynamism through the use of discretion-sensitive masks (silhouettes) intuitively protecting layer data privacy through robust established models.

Advanced encryption methods where algorithm performance and complexity, along with redundancy strategies, are compensated within asymmetric multi-key lock techniques are critical. NATO and many other international cooperative governmental structures have bilateral mutual trust agreements that provide deep autonomous loops. Strict adherence to privacy provisions across multi-jurisdictional boundaries through seal-based technology underpin cross-enterprise collaborative performances modelling the achieved bordering agreements guaranteeing sophisticated compliance through the act of sealed integrations driven towards confidential through-proxy-based routers.

Scalability remains equally important concerning deployment. Adaptability within translation services is of utmost importance concerning future sustainability, as they must be able to process exponentially increasing amounts of data and meet more intricate linguistic needs. Effective allocation of resources and load balancing mechanisms have a decisive impact on handling complex workflows or increasing operational demands and optimising performance during changing demand levels. Additionally, the use of cloud computing technology and distributed systems can provide the required scalability for efficient continuous cross-lingual communication and analysis.

From a procedural perspective, creating a clearly defined operational protocol is a necessity. Strategies set for upkeep, maintenance, system updates, and incident response not only improve operational efficiency but strengthen the overall resilience of the translation infrastructure. Management of translation systems security is significantly improved by standardised methods for user authentication enforcement, audit trail documentation, and real-time activity monitoring, allowing proactive identification and mitigation of potential weaknesses.

Furthermore, the integration of other intelligence tools and the incorporation of other technologies of intelligence systems require careful implementation of pre-existing security protocols. Companies can implement best practices of the industry and follow security policies while enhancing their translation solutions, making sure that they will function properly within the entire ecosystem of intelligence tools and platforms. The need for cross-lingual NLP bolsters intelligence capabilities which can be demonstrated with the seamless engagement with language-centric analytics and the domain-oriented workflows.

Clearly, the complex issues around regulatory policy that ensure secure and scalable translation solutions require an all-encompassing solution that integrates technical, procedural, and legal workflows. While focusing on data protection, scalability, and compliance with policies during deployment, intelligence agencies will be able to improve their cross-lingual capabilities and foster better communications and understanding among linguistically diverse sources of intelligence.

The Road Ahead: Future Trends in Cross-Lingual NLP and Their Implications

Technological progress promises to transform cross-lingual natural language processing (NLP) into a tool capable of communication and information exchange at a global scale. It is this promise that drives this chapter, dedicated to outlining possible trends within cross-lingual NLP and their emerging consequences.

One of the most exciting NLP cross-lingual prospects is achieving better integration of multilingual NLP models with advanced learning algorithms, allowing more accurate and fluent comprehension and generation of human languages. Also remarkable is the NLP convergence with other emerging technologies like augmented and virtual realities which present novel opportunities for more immersive cross-lingual experiences beyond education, commerce, and entertainment.

Along with many challenging questions, cross-lingual NLP entails important and urgent ethical concerns. From this perspective, bias, fairness, and privacy issues within the scope of cross-lingual NLP system design and implementation are some critical aspects that need to be addressed. Proactively ensuring inclusivity and diversity of language representation within the frameworks of NLP will help promote equal opportunities for accessing controlled information and services among disparate language communities.

Another important trajectory in cross-lingual NLP deals with the fragmentation problem in resource-poor languages. With advances in technology, there is increasing attention towards providing NLP features for languages which have been marginalised for too long in NLP research and applications. The NLP functionalities for these languages can be empowered through transfer learning and language agnostic pre-training to level these languages' resource deficits.

In addition, the use of NMT opens up new possibilities with cross-lingual NLP. New models and methods are expected to improve translation for difficult and context-rich language pairs. Knowledge graphs combined with cross-lingual NLP will provide better understanding and integration of different languages and cultures.

The ramifications of these advancing trends stretch far from the academic and industrial spheres, which are deeply profound. These trends can foster greater integrative collaboration across cultures and foster understanding beyond language barriers. Furthermore, the impact of cross-lingual NLP in international relations and issues pertaining to conflict resolution and humanitarian aid will be increasingly crucial as it progresses. This will foster greater dialogue and understanding between diverse cultures. In other words, the future of cross-lingual NLP promises remarkable innovations anchored in social responsibility and unbounded opportunity for reshaping global connectivity and inclusivity.

7

The Power of LLMs

Large Language Models in Intelligence Analysis

Introduction to Large Language Models: Capabilities and Scope

Advancements in Natural Language Processing (NLP) through the development of large language models (LLMs) have widened the scope for leveraging powerful text understanding tools. Their ability to transform raw data into useful information precisely augments their utility in critical domains such as intelligence analysis. LLMs improve the methods that are available for deriving insights from unstructured data. These models provide sophisticated analytical capabilities to process data from diverse and complex sources like news articles, social media posts, and academic publications. Unlike older systems that relied on simple heuristic keyword matching or parsing based on rigid grammar rules, LLMs go further than that and make it possible for analysts to address the deep contextual subtleties entwined within language. Such models are able to analyse vast volumes of linguistic data, identify patterns, infer meanings, and formulate context-appropriate responses. Therefore, LLMs greatly assist intelligence analysts in extracting critical insights from massive volumes of data and identifying important patterns with unparalleled accuracy and speed. LLMs also tend to work remarkably well across many regions, languages, dialects, and other sociolinguistic varieties of known languages, aiding by responding to communication barriers and offering multilingual analysis.

This versatility is especially important in the scope of global intelligence with multilingual data sources as a point of concern. The functions of LLMs extend past understanding a language since they can also aid in the generation of texts, summarising them automatically, and translating them in context which deepens the analytic toolkit available to intelligence professionals. While discussing the possible uses of LLMs in regard to intelligence analysis, it is clear these models are quite revolutionary, altering established practices and driving progress in how information is analysed, processed, and shared.

Historical Evolution: From RNNs to Transformer Architectures

Recurrent Neural Networks (RNNs) represented the earliest attempt at sequence modelling in the context of natural language processing (NLP). These networks offered insights into how to capture context and dependencies in sequential data due to their capacity to remember and use data from previous inputs. However, RNNs faced challenges due to fundamental shortcomings, particularly the inability to effectively capture long-range dependencies due to the vanishing gradient problem. The increasing sophistication required from language models led to the emergence of Long Short-Term Memory (LSTM) networks, which improved traditional RNNs by enhancing memory capabilities and learning temporal patterns. However, the evolutionary breakthrough came with the introduction of Transformer models, which fundamentally changed the approach to NLP. Self-attention techniques were integrated into RNN-based models; thus, global dependencies were effectively captured by the model. Transformers, developed by Vaswani et al. in 2017, became revolutionary and further advanced modelling language, serving as the foundation upon which powerful large language models (LLMs) were built.

The Transformer's ability to capture long-range dependencies and contextual information without sequential limitations is what led to its adoption in many NLP applications such as machine translation, document summarisation, and sentiment analysis. The introduction of pre-trained GPT (Generative Pre-trained Transformer) and BERT (Bidirectional Encoder Representations from Transformers) further cemented the place of Transformer architectures in the field of NLP. These pre-trained models enabled transfer learning with fine-tuning, yielding substantial improvements in performance on various downstream tasks, which brought LLMs to the centre of intelligence analysis and decision-making. The shift from RNNs to Transformer models marks a history of constant refinement in search of better language modelling techniques, which LLMs have now fundamentally transformed in the context of intelligence analysis and many other fields.

LLMs in Action: Practical Applications within Intelligence Analysis

The use of Large Language Models (LLMs) has proven invaluable in the sphere of intelligence analysis by processing and interpreting large amounts of unstructured text data. LLMs capable of advanced natural language comprehension and translation, like GPT-3, BERT, and T5, have become indispensable in enhancing the workflow of analytical tasks in intelligence agencies.

Information extraction and entity recognition are two of the more popular LLM applications. Reputation systems, user profiling, social network analysis, and online monitoring are carried out using these models by enabling them to automatically identify and extract vital components of complete texts such as names of people, organisations, locations and dates using deep contextual understanding of language.

Furthermore, LLMs have proven useful in conducting sentiment analysis which helps gauge the general public mood, evaluate perceptions concerning a particular event or person, as well as uncover possible risks and threats to security, including emergent trends. Using these models to interpret language reveals even the most sophisticated details regarding sentiment analysis which are needed for threat evaluation and planning strategies.

LLM technology also assists users in document summarisation and clustering; hence, they aid in eliminating the difficult task of going through long reports, articles, and even open source intelligence. With the use of summarisation, these models are able to transform massive volumes of text into small pieces which are easier to digest. This way, users will have access to important details without navigating through a lot of data and overwhelming information. Also, with the clustering methods available in LLMs, they greatly enhance the ability to automatically assign documents into different themes in order to organise them to help analysts identify patterns and relationships among various sources.

Of great importance is that LLMs, when integrated with predictive analytics, are extremely useful in forecasting something such as geopolitical developments, economic activities, and social changes. Based on the large contextual information stored in these models, the analysts' reasoning exercises to envision and evaluate several scenarios pertaining to the set objectives and outcomes makes it possible to take informed decisions within intelligence analysis due to better historical precedents, geopolitical relations, and socio-economic markers.

To summarise, the important uses of LLMs in intelligence analysis permeate a variety of essential activities from extraction, sentiment assessment, and summarisation to prediction and analysis. Increasingly sophisticated LLMs will hybridise intelligence workflows, revolutionising the whole range of analysis techniques and greatly improving the productivity and impact of intelligence activities.

Enhancing Analytical Precision: Understanding Context and Nuance

The application of advanced language models has transformed the field of intelligence analysis by improving analytical accuracy with a profound comprehension of context and detail. With the adoption of LLMs by intelligence agencies, it becomes increasingly important to analyse text with precision at different levels of semantics. The focus here is on how LLMs resolve nuanced semantics and, thereby, improve the precision of intelligence analysis.

Context refers to a complex dimension of meaning which has considerable bearing on the interpretation of one's information. Recognition of context makes LLMs masters in understanding speech as they pay attention to proverbs as well as jokes and phrases that have been modified from their original format. Such models can not only expose depths of concealed intent but also determine subtler implications, which are most often ignored by traditional analytical approaches, due to the context in which information is presented. With this powerful grasp of intelligence data and diverse sources, the analyst's insights have moved beyond capturing the surface of intelligence data.

Additionally, the capability of an LLM to grasp nuanced details is critical in understanding the intricacies of intelligence reports and other necessary texts, such as international letters. LLMs help intelligence specialists unravel the thick web of contexts that characterise the world in important geopolitical debates and ambiguous utterances.

In the case of a certain culture or region, words that may have special meanings elsewhere could mean something entirely different there. In consideration of varying conventions and dialects, LLMs can provide more sophisticated analysis of multicultural intelligence, deeper comprehension, as well as more flexibility with changing modes of discourse. Adequate comprehension of sophisticated language also guarantees that no piece of detail or implication is neglected. This allows for powerful analysis acquired through communications done in different languages and through various socio-cultural lenses.

To summarise, the combination of a contextual understanding of the material alongside a profound appreciation for the details of language intricately equips large language models (LLMs) to assist tremendously in activities requiring deep analysis and precision. With these tools, intelligence analysts are able to masterfully reinterpret subtle contextual and linguistic intricacies, enabling them to enhance sophisticated accuracy in multipolar global environments, which in turn amplifies strategic decision-making.

Real-World Case Studies: LLMs Transforming Intelligence Workflows

Through the use of Large Language Models (LLMs), systems that process data are deepening their understanding of intricate linguistic sources. This allows firms to obtain useful data from their unstructured text documents, which in turn enhances automated decision-making processes; this epitomises the advanced natural language processing solutions of modern days. We do not need to look very far for proof of transformational LLMs impacts on the actionable intelligence domains as real-world case studies are readily available. For instance, one LLM case study suggests that counter-terrorism units can now intercept millions of multi-lingual and multimodal texts, social media posts, and other forms of communications and sift through for threatening signals. Analysts using LLMs in these scenarios have come to appreciate how faster distillation of pertinent information is now possible to reveal elusive dependent and independent variables. LLMs are also used in the financial domains including in the analyses of financial intelligence where they assist analysts in anomaly detection which deals with the identification of abnormal patterns in transactions. This has expanded the capabilities of financial forensic units especially in fighting sophisticated financial crimes like white-collar crimes or money laundering.

Moreover, LLMs have shown usefulness in geopolitical forecasting by analysing and synthesising large volumes of news articles, reports, and diplomatic communications to offer detailed perspectives on shifting global dynamics. Furthermore, monitoring and evaluating possible security risks within certain areas geographically has been augmented by the use of LLMs alongside satellite imagery data. These case studies highlight the profound impact that LLMs have in reshaping intelligence frameworks, equipping analysts with tools to manage the intricacies of today's information landscape with unmatched accuracy and speed.

Resource Management: Balancing Accuracy, Speed, and Computational Cost

The management of resources is becoming increasingly important as government intelligence operations begin to extensively use LLMs (Large Language Models) for various analytical purposes. Accuracy, speed, and computational cost are all quintessential LLM requirements which, when mastered, will increase workflow efficiency in LLM-powered intelligence frameworks.

Optimal resource management in this respect includes the operational models adopted, LLM selection, and hardware infrastructure to be utilised. The LLM chosen must correspond best to the task at hand because of the model dimension which includes the training dataset, and the fine-tuning prerequisite. There are trade-offs between accuracy and computational demand for resources and having a good grasp of an intelligence analysis application's parameters is helpful.

Understanding the computational burden placed by these LLMs requires associated robust hardware infrastructure. Proper cloud computing assets paired alongside high performing computers greatly aid in the absorption of LLMs in existing intelligence frameworks. It is also important to ensure that optimised hardware setups are considered for these frameworks so that there is an equilibrium between the speed of processing and cost.

Similarly, operational systems form the backbone of resource management. The effective implementation of workflows that avoid unnecessary steps, make the most out of concurrent processing, and take full advantage of caching can considerably enhance the performance of LLMs. Moreover, sustained oversight of resource allocation and performance metrics enables intelligence agencies to make infrastructure changes on the go, adapting in real time.

The balance between accuracy, speed, and the cost of computation transcends the realm of technology into that of strategy and policy. Agency analysts and leaders grapple with the opportunity cost that comes with improved accuracy as it demands additional computational resources and time for processing. Aligning priorities against resources for analysis ensures that LLMs are used optimally and conservatively for the long term.

Resilient adaptation to shifting technological paradigms and resource limitations stems from the refined use of LLMs, making resource management all the more critical. By strategically managing resources, intelligence agencies stand to enhance their LLM utilisation while reducing operational challenges and improving strategic analytical performance.

Integrating LLMs with Existing Analytical Frameworks: Best Practices

Intelligence practitioners face both opportunities and challenges when incorporating Large Language Models (LLMs) within established analytical frameworks. Analysts have the potential to leverage LLMs to further their understanding and skill in unlocking pertinent information from extensive volumes of unstructured textual data.

However, the unobstructed adoption of LLMs entails a multifaceted approach that balances their implementation within existing analytic practices.

Strategic frameworks for the adoption of LLMs into pre-existing infrastructures need to assess model compatibility and the overall interoperability with the organisation's architecture. These considerations include, amongst others, the potential for expansion, the available options for execution, and the computational power needed to reach optimised efficiency. Furthermore, preset strategies describing automation of core analytic tasks like data cleaning, model training, and evaluation of results need to be designed to enable smooth adoption with controlled change to established practices.

Best practices technology policies advocate for the implementation of comprehensive training and upskilling programmes to enable the effective use of LLMs by analysts. Due to the fast-paced evolution of the models themselves, and the growing field of natural language processing, continuous learning and skill acquisition is necessary to maximise the utility of LLMs in intelligence analysis. Organisations should adopt integrated training approaches that combine classroom instruction with practical training to enable analysts to master the integration of LLMs with ease and expertise.

Furthermore, the use of LLMs comes with ethical and privacy implications, especially with regards to sensitive or classified data. Databased best practices stress the need for strong governance and compliance with legal frameworks to minimise risks concerning data privacy, discrimination, and access. Implementation of clear rules around model assessment, validation, and accountability is also necessary to strengthen trust in the LLM-based analytics and therefore enhance their intelligence agency wide acceptability and usability.

Lastly, integration practices highlight the importance of cultivating collaboration and peer-to-peer dissemination of knowledge among interdisciplinary groups. It is evident that optimising integration goes beyond the technical dimensions as it requires collaboration, comprehensive communication, and multiple rounds of refinements based on feedback from various contributors. An ideal blend of LLM proficiency and expertise within particular fields allows organisations to utilise advanced language models integrated with classical models for more precise and profound reasoning in a continuous cycle of knowledge reciprocation.

To put it differently, integrating LLMs within existing frameworks requires an alignment between organisational goals, ethical boundaries, socio-structural imperatives, and human factors - all approached through a multi-faceted angle. Intelligence practitioners must embrace transformative change while achieving technological integration by adhering to organisational change leadership principles and fostering a culture of robust adaptability, creativity, and best practice benchmarks.

Challenges and Limitations: Addressing Bias and Interpretability

The introduction and proliferation of Large Language Models (LLMs) have changed the landscape of intelligence analysis as analysts are now able to analyse immense amounts of unstructured data with a high level of precision. However, the great power towards information processing and sense-making provided by LLMs comes alongside the responsibilities of resolving issues pertaining to their limitations, especially bias and interpretability. Training data bias is one of the primary concerns with LLMs; Biases, such as underrepresentation, can inject unfair algorithms into the outcome of the analysis. LLMs are trained on historical datasets, which means they extract information based on datasets that might contain some form of societal biases. Intelligence analysts need to address these biases—acknowledge them and make deliberate attempts to avoid them—so that their conclusions do not end up being filtered through biased lenses. Moreover, the ability to trace back conclusions to their constituent parts is critical in the LLM-generation process as this preserves accountability and trust in the analytical process. Given the intricacy of the LLMs, it is often difficult to comprehend the manner in which they reach conclusions. This is a challenge for the analysts because the models are black boxes, and results verification is often impossible devoid of unmasking the internal mechanisms of the models. The same gaps of understandability make explaining the importance of assessments and accompanying information to stakeholders and decision makers very problematic. The lack of explanatory power adds a challenge on its own without considering the described concerns.

Overcoming these challenges necessitates a combination of different strategies. To begin with, addressing issues such as bias within the training datasets demands strict processes for data curation. Advocating model bias mitigation with diverse perspective consideration and discrimination pattern minimisation can also be achieved using adversarial training and fairness constraints. Additionally, using LLMs interpretable by constructing explanation methods of predictions through attention and saliency maps increases transparency of the analytical process. Domain experts, ethicists, and data scientists need to work together to establish comprehensive ethical ranges and best practices on the use and application of LLMs in intelligence analysis. Challenging LLM-derived insights has the potential to undermine ethical credibility and erode trust in the models.

Evolving Threats: Counter-AI Measures and Adversarial Learning

The world of information intelligence receives an overhaul in how large language models (LLMs) can process and interpret data. Alongside these evolving capabilities, emerging threats to AI and NLP systems pose an equally pressing concern. These threats specifically include counter-AI measures and the adversarial learning techniques designed to exploit weaknesses in LLMs and autonomous systems. Intelligence professionals need to understand these evolving threats to fortify the reliability and trustworthiness of their analytical outputs.

A broad array of strategies falls under the umbrella of counter-AI measures which focus on the manipulation and circumventing of functions within an LLM. There are always those who, for one reason or another, work against the collective good and seek to use sophisticated model poisoning, data tampering, or targeted attacks to undermine the trust of these models. Without a doubt, as LLMs permeate various intelligence functions, nefarious attempts at the sophistication of natural language processing algorithms become more commonplace. This knowledge should catalyse the need to impose proactive mechanisms and robust security protocols tailored towards mitigating the impact of adversarial efforts.

Adversarial learning extends into AI and machine learning, primarily examining ways to comprehend and defend against evolving dangers to AI technologies. It is the process of modelling attack scenarios and building robust systems designed to endure hostile inputs. For LLMs, adversaries may attempt to apply certain input modifications to predict incorrectly or influence the result through complex output patterns. By comprehensively studying these options and implementing corresponding counter-strategies, an intelligence analyst can strengthen the application of LLMs and safeguard their frameworks from potential exploitation.

Moreover, the application of AI and security highlights the pressing need to bring together scholars from artificial intelligence, cyber security, and intelligence analysis. It addresses the need to create adaptive defences and share threat intelligence to continually improve protection strategies for LLM and other NLP systems. Intelligence agencies can defend the integrity of their analytical infrastructure while maintaining the rigorous benchmarks of precision and reliability critical for informed decisions by fostering a proactive framework designed to confront adversarial threats.

With each passing day, the continuous clash of competing sides with new technologies makes adaptability especially important. For LLM-based intelligence frameworks, the ability to predict and respond to counterstrategy actions is critical in maintaining their functionality and usefulness. Professionals operating in this field must be allowed the flexibility to implement their entire toolbox, which includes creativity and constant technological advances, collaboration across domains, as well as perpetual monitoring to scan for possible new threats or changes in classical ones.

Conclusion: The Future Landscape of Intelligence Analysis Empowered by LLMs

The advancement of Large Language Models (LLMs) has brought new transformational changes in the intelligence analysis field, unlocking new potential for actionable insight discovery and providing increased capability to analyse massive amounts of unstructured data. Evolving intelligence providers would need to appreciate both the challenges and opportunities unattended within their ever-growing domains. The impacts of imbuing LLMs into systems of intelligence could be summarised in a few pivotal points. To begin with, LLMs come with the ability to comprehend multiple languages alongside providing unprecedented text retrieval capabilities, meaning that analysts are able to cut through the signals with extreme precision and at breakneck speeds. Also, the scope of applying LLMs shifted the boundary of analytical types. It enabled the use of language context in the analysis of sentiment, entity resolution, and thematic categorisation. All in all, LLMs transformed systems of intelligence by equipping analysts with multi-speaking and reading capability thus enabling them to see and understand beyond the linguistic and semantic curtains. Nonetheless, these temptations bring troublesome challenges of adversarial learning and bias distortion, which invoke the deep scrutiny and reinforcement of models.

Moreover, with LLMs laying the groundwork for profound change, centralised issues of ethics like privacy, transparency, and accountability require careful handling. If we consider the shift that LLMs will have on the scope of intelligence analysis, the landscape is painted with unbounded potential balanced by the demand for perpetual surveillance as well as ethical management. We see a radical shift for now brought by the collision between human creativity and machine intelligence which creates new frontiers of symbiotic partnership, redefining the scope of analytics. It calls for intelligence practitioners to navigate the course that advances in technology while keeping strong the anchor of ethics, aiming to leverage the evocative promise of LLMs to strengthen security in the world and promote societal well-being.

Countering Deception

NLP for Disinformation, Misinformation, and Propaganda Detection

Introduction to Information Disorder: Definitions and Challenges

In the digital landscape of today, one of the paramount concerns is information disorder. It includes disinformation, misinformation, and malinformation, each posing different challenges to social and political life alongside security. Effectively mitigating these negative consequences requires grappling with the nuances of these concepts. Information disorder, in essence, describes an attempt or acts of willful disseminating and publishing false or misleading information intended to harm the public good. Even so, information disorder lacks universally accepted definitions, which has made this sophisticated matter even more complex. The multifaceted problem of information disorder is compounded by the unprecedented speed coupled with the scale of the amount of information people share online, the echo chamber phenomenon in social media, sophisticated opinion manipulation tactics, the blurring between the realms of real news and opinions versus deliberate falsehoods, and more. Comprehending the problem holistically is crucial for developing effective detection and intervention methods. Any adopted definition shapes the strategy for detection and mitigative efforts.

For example, distinguishing misinformation as the unknowing spread of information and disinformation as its intentional counterpart requires separate analytical frameworks. The same goes for understanding malinformation which deals with the sharing of authentic information for harmful purposes, requiring specific detection methodologies. Therefore, developing effective counteraction strategies depends on a clear and thorough grasp of the multifaceted nature of information disorder. With the understanding of the definitions and intricacies of information disorder, intelligence analysts and policymakers would be able to develop effective adaptive strategies to mitigate its harm and safeguard the information ecosystem while strengthening societal resilience against deceit.

The Psychology of Deception: Understanding Cognitive Vulnerabilities

Cognitive vulnerabilities can easily be exploited for perception and judgment domains. Particularly understanding psychology deception can help to counteract propaganda, misinformation, and disinformation. Cognitive vulnerabilities in human beings are discussed in these pages, with an emphasis on psychological mechanisms that predispose individuals to the deceptive information. The human mind is susceptible to numerous influences such as biases and heuristics, emotional effects, as well as social groups. These human elements affect the processing of information. Reasoning, recall, reinterpreting, as well as memory retrieval is framed by cognitive biases such as confirmation bias and availability heuristic. Thinking is also influenced by emotions whereby the rational component loses its grip over the ability to think clearly. Moreover, social influence dynamics such as conformity and authority can lead to lowering the standard of judgment one places on their actions. Examining these cognitive vulnerabilities enables analysts and researchers to understand the psychological processes behind deception.

Recognising these vulnerabilities supports the creation of NLP-based solutions to reduce the impacts of disinformation and propaganda. Additionally, applying the relationship of cognitive vulnerabilities to deceptive content assists in the crafting strategy of targeted instruction and advocacy programmes to improve media literacy and critical thinking. In the fight against disinformation, recognising and strategically managing cognitive vulnerabilities is an essential component toward fortifying the public against manipulative framing and narrative warfare.

NLP Techniques for Identifying Misinformation Patterns

In the area of intelligence and information studies, the spread of misinformation can be quite problematic. Solving such a problem requires sophisticated natural language processing techniques for detection and pattern recognition. One basic such NLP technique is sentiment analysis. Sentiment analysis captures emotions, opinions and attitudes expressed in text. Analysts can interpret the sentiment regarding certain content and gauge the chances of underlying bias or deceptive messaging. Another important technique is named entity recognition which includes detecting and classifying entities as organisations, peoples and locations cited in the text. By associating the entities with their credibility and known sources, analysts can trace and verify the potential sources and connections of misinformation. Moreover, topic modelling and document clustering are important for identifying patterns of false narratives and so covert coordinated disinformation. They help detect flow of themes and recurrent language over multiple documents contributing to the detection of orchestrated efforts towards disinformation. Besides, the use of machine translation along with cross-lingual NLP examines discrepancies and inconsistencies in translated texts revealing possible distortions and manipulations.

Furthermore, large language models and sophisticated natural language processing (NLP) techniques help to identify linguistic irregularities and abnormally structured language typical of deceptive documents. NLP models are also capable of identifying more nuanced differences in the way language is used and indicate edited or fabricated information. Finally, the use of NLP aids in providing a holistic picture of the context and metadata related to the content and gives information on how it could have been manipulated and the pathways through which such manipulation might have occurred. The application of such NLP methods provides critical capabilities for intelligence analysts to determine, evaluate, and counteract the impact of pervasive disinformation within the contemporary information environment.

Strategies for Propaganda Analysis: Unveiling Hidden Agendas

Untangling propaganda is a complex problem confronting intelligence analysts that requires a great deal of effort and focus. We focus on the theories and techniques in the process of propaganda analysis. The main aim of propaganda is to shape perception, belief, and behaviour, often acting through the covert distribution of half-truths or lies. Countering such machinations requires a coordinated approach integrating sociolinguistic, psychological, and anthropological aspects. Coded and biased linguistic expressions of propaganda require professional decoding to provide context. Furthermore, the cognitive biases and psychological tricks used by propagandists provide great aid in dismantling their narratives. History, politics, and society offer context to the rationale behind more aggressive strategies of propaganda campaigns to determine their intended purpose. Combining all these factors gives analysts the means to reveal concealed concepts and plans devised by propagandists. There is a systematic approach to detecting propaganda using advanced NLP methods such as sentiment analysis, entity recognition, and contextual interpretation. In addition, sophisticated patterns of language and ideology that are woven into narratives that are purposely deceptive can be exposed through large language models.

Nevertheless, understanding the shifts in tactics and strategies used in propaganda is equally important as recognising its fluid nature. Thus, keeping situational awareness of changing propaganda frameworks requires due diligence and adaptive strategies. Case studies along with actual instances help to concretely illustrate effective propaganda analysis, showcasing successful and unsuccessful strategies in past engagements. In the end, mastering propaganda analysis requires a blend of critical thinking and technical skills with an intimate grasp of socio-cultural frameworks. With these factors in place, propaganda can be countered and the integrity of information protected, thereby ensuring national security.

Leveraging Large Language Models for Deceptive Content Detection

Within the context of analytical intelligence, the content detection needs to be supplemented with modern technologies in what is called content detection automation. This problem can be resolved using Large Language Models (LLMs) like GPT-3 and BERT, which can significantly improve the understanding and detection of disinformation, misinformation, and propaganda. The advanced LLMs have recently shown unprecedented sophistication in understanding and generating language, hence a desperate need to exploit those for countering deceitful narratives. When powered with LLMs, analysts can use LLMs for artificial intelligence in processing natural languages to analyse texts on a scale and depth that was impossible before, rapidly flagging lexicons portraying bias, manipulation, and so-called anomalies. LLMs' abilities to grasp the context, subtleties, and the changing face of the language make it possible to detect some very sharp sudden changes and inconsistencies in meanings that are likely to be deceitful. Incorporation of LLMs into workflows enables intelligence analysts to dramatically enhance their ability to sift through massive troves of information and analyse thousands of previously hidden misinformation or disinformation. Beyond that, the learning processes integrated into LLMs allow for learning with changes in deceptive tactics as well, thus keeping the tactics always updated and timeless.

Moreover, large language models enable the expansion of tackling deceptive content in different languages and analysing global narratives and propaganda in various languages. This is vital especially today in the digital world where cross-lingual disinformation poses a threat to geopolitical order and social stability. Further, the sophisticated processing of LLMs may contribute to explaining the psycholinguistic factors in the deceptive content, hence providing explanations on the psychological systems involved in audience manipulations. With the advancements of LLMs core technologies, there is the possibility to further improve the recognition and the response to deceptive content which could radically change the approaches to countering disorder information. At the same time, however, we must address and take action on the ethical impacts and biases that come with using LLMs technology on credibility checks and classification of deceptive and fraudulent content. Finding the balance between progress and responsible use of technologies will invite possibilities of using LLMs to their full potential while avoiding negative outcomes.

With the growing influence of LLMs and an understanding of their ethical implications, intelligence agencies stand to enhance their safeguards against misleading information and build greater resilience to sophisticated deceptive content, fostering fortitude against changing hostile tactics.

Evaluating the Reliability of Sources: NLP-Driven Fact-Checking

The abundance of information available today can make evaluating source credibility a daunting challenge in intelligence studies, especially in the face of disinformation strategies. An essential aspect of an analyst's NLP toolkit is fact verification using Natural Language Processing, which applies computational language and machine learning techniques for parsing and verifying the claims made in texts from different documents. Algorithms systematically analyse the words and the context in which they are used in order to detect inaccuracies, biases, or lies. A vital NLP fact verification component is reconceptualisation of credibility indicators and their weighting within the text. These may include: rhetoric structure, sentiment polarity, reputation of the author, coherence and cohesion of the text's subject matter, and reliability of the statements made in relation to the temporal context. Sophisticated models of NLP are capable of detecting an ill-formed untrustworthy utterance, thereby safeguarding analysts' evaluations regarding the credibility of the information. Besides, through automation of many document analyses, NLP enhances information consolidation and provides synthesised overviews for efficient comparison to ascertain fact triangulation, highlighting differences or inconsistencies.

This approach enables better understanding of misleading narratives and helps analysts form a cohesive understanding of multifaceted events. Addressing the challenges posed by disinformation campaigns across multiple platforms also requires NLP-driven fact checking. As malicious actors revise their strategies to exploit weaknesses across various channels of communication, NLP has the capability to synthesise data from social media, traditional news outlets, and other public forums.

Such an approach aids in identifying unreliable sources in addition to enhancing source evaluation by allowing analysts to track the spread of deceptive content. In time, decisions taken by intelligence agencies could be informed by real-time fact-checking done via NLP which would aid in timely response and preemptive actions targeted at manipulating information streams. Still, the ethics of employing NLP for determining a source's credibility need to be addressed urgently. Privacy concerns, social injustices related to bias in algorithms, and the safeguarding of classified details demands careful scrutiny from analysts. The conflict between individual rights and the quest for truth presents a perennial tension when NLP is deployed for fact checking. That said, employing NLP in the stringent assessment of source credibility underscores the fact that intelligence analysis can be fortified against disinformation and enhanced by rigorous evaluation.

Cross-Platform Disinformation: Integrating Multi-Source Data

Contemporary interconnected digital systems and networks have exponentially complicated the spread of disinformation, significantly affecting intelligence analysis and national security. In order to construct an understanding of the phenomenon of cross-platform disinformation, it is necessary to integrate data from multiple sources and employ various strategies. In this section, I will focus on the issues around cross-platform disinformation and explain how multi-source data can be used to counter deceptive narratives.

Social media, news agencies, online discussion forums and other channels of electronic communication are just a few examples of disparate platforms that contain information data relevant for a specific purpose. Integration of multiple sources aids in tracking and monitoring the spread of disinformation as well as its transformations in different online ecosystems. Integrated multi-source data also help determine the presence of orchestrated disinformation designed to influence and disrupt public or social systems of delicate balance.

It is easier to carry out cross-platform disinformation analyses using natural language processing (nLP) techniques. NLP algorithms are capable of processing large amounts of free text from different sources, identifying linguistic patterns, and drawing key insights to expose anomalies associated with disinformation. Moreover, sentiment analysis and topic modelling are essential in determining what the emotions and themes around a particular piece of disinformation text at a given period across different platforms.

The development of disinformation and ways of tracking them can be understood through various analytic dimensions enabled by NLP, which reveal intricate relationships in multi-source datasets.

As any other form of discourse, disinformation can be addressed from a linguistic perspective. Besides using the linguistic data, it is necessary to include multi-source data coupled with advanced visualisation and network analysis techniques. The interconnectedness of disinformation across different platforms paints a more complete picture regarding its dissemination and propagation patterns. Network analysis enables the mapping of influential nodes and the identification of echo chambers where disinformation can thrive unchecked. By employing advanced visualisation techniques in multi-source data sets, intelligence agencies are able to trace the origin of disinformation, its diffusion pathways, and devise targeted countermeasures.

Cross-platform disinformation remains a challenge due to the collaborative silos of intelligence agencies, tech companies, and academic researchers. With defined boundaries for collaboration and the exchange of data, multi-source data would provide a more thorough approach to digital deception, harnessing different fields of expertise.

To sum up, complex disinformation systems transcending multiple platforms require sophisticated frameworks.

Using NLP-powered analytics alongside advanced visualisation techniques and collaborative frameworks, agencies can improve their capacity to identify, assess, and address the effects of deceptive counter narratives in multilevel digitally integrated spaces.

Real-Time Monitoring Systems: Technologies and Methodologies

The proliferation of disinformation and propaganda on numerous digital platforms requires the immediate development of real-time monitoring systems that utilise modern technologies and methodologies. These systems are vital for proactive detection and mitigation of misleading content by intelligence agencies and organisations in order to protect information ecosystems. Real-time monitoring refers to the ongoing collection and analysis of multiple data streams, including social media, news outlets, online discussion platforms, and other pertinent channels.

The importance of artificial intelligence, alongside natural language processing (NLP) and machine learning, are vital when it comes to real-time monitoring. NLP technologies can identify deceptive content's tell-tale suspicious patterns, keywords, and even sentiment analysis in large textual corpora and across languages. Content can also be automatically categorised according to preset parameters using machine learning algorithms, making it easier to prioritise high-risk information that requires human intervention. Moreover, tools powered by AI can adjust to shifting disinformation strategies continuously, which improves the effectiveness of real-time monitoring systems.

Strategies concerning real-time monitoring consist of automated algorithms, manual analysis, combined with a human touch specialising in the relevant field. Algorithms automatically scan and sort a majority of the incoming data, selecting some for deeper examination which include content that is erroneous and might be misleading. Linguistic analysis works on the textual data as it examines the meaning of words and inconsistency within context helps in revealing hidden agendas of propaganda and misinformation. Besides, there is a need for a person in the loop for contextualising alerts that the computer systems generate, providing expertise and specialist information which adds value to the monitoring process.

Moreover, sophisticated data visualisation and analytics techniques are useful for monitoring in real time. With these tools, analysts are able to detect the emergence of disinformation trends, monitor their amplification networks, and track how deceptive narratives are transmitted through online systems. Visualising complex interconnected webs through which disinformation campaigns operate helps analysts to understand the propagation dynamics of campaigns and tailor counter strategies.

In summary, the construction and application of technologies and methodologies for real-time monitoring serve as a more proactive approach to defending against disinformation and propaganda. This chapter has emphasised the crucial importance of NLP, machine learning, linguistic analysis, AI, human intelligence, and advanced visualisation in reinforcing real-time monitoring capabilities. Enhanced information ecosystems that withstand attacks of disinformation are, in turn, more effective intelligence tools in combating the pervasive threat of manipulative content.

Case Studies: Lessons Learned from Historical and Recent Events

A case study examination provides insights on the application of NLP techniques to counter disinformation campaigns. Historical events, like wartime propaganda and the dissemination of false narratives via traditional media, underscore the enduring issue of misinformation and provide a foundational understanding. From an NLP perspective, there is a far-reaching value for intelligence analysts in recognising patterns, strategies, and tactics used by malicious actors in their information operations. These patterns and strategies make it possible to design specific approaches for detection and neutralisation that adapt to information warfare's changing environments.

Examining recent events also emphasises the problem posed by the evolving digital context. The advent of social media has accelerated and amplified the deceptive content's access and attribution, making it increasingly difficult to differentiate between original and doctored information. Fostered by powerful disinformation campaigns, cyber-enabled influence operations, and orchestrated propaganda bursts, modern deception has grown in complexity. Understanding these contemporary occurrences enables practitioners to comprehend the evolving malevolent tactics and technology which inform the needed refinements of NLP combat systems.

One example of a case study that can be looked at is how a variety of different forms of disinformation campaigns may interfere with democratic activities. Analysts can reconstruct the web of lies and identify the flaws in the societal communication systems that are exploited by deceitful messaging through analysing cases where elections are compromised using false narratives as well as tailored messages. Analysts are able to use NLP to examine the language and context of deceitful messages to create early detection systems and counteractive strategies that protect democratic institutions from manipulative attacks.

One of the issues that must be studied further is in the field of public health and safety. The spread of misinformation in healthcare has proven to have a negative impact on global society in the most recent example of a worldwide pandemic. Analysts are able to protect information ecosystems by studying the spread of false medical advice, conspiracy theories, and phony news during times of public health emergencies in order to actively eliminate the harmful disinformation and deceptive narratives aimed at the safety and security of the people. This helps ensure the active detection and elimination of hostile narratives that endanger the health and safety of people.

A complete examination of past and contemporary case studies integrates theory with practice, enhancing understanding of the landscapes of disinformation. With these lessons, intelligence specialists leverage the game-changing capabilities of NLP to construct unbreakable shields against deceptive narratives while preserving the integrity of information ecosystems.

Ethical Considerations in Disinformation Detection

As is the case with any emerging technological field, ethical issues are especially critical in terms of disinformation detection due to the societal consequences that can stem from the "cancellation" of content. The algorithmic tools that address misinformation issues through natural language processing (NLP) techniques pose interesting dilemmas that sit on the ethical spectrum. A primary issue in the ethical spectrum is the trade-off between privacy and security. Disinformation detection necessitates the collection and analysis of massive data sets, which must remain within lawful and moral boundaries of data privacy laws.

The careful management of data draws a line regarding the balance between information ethics and social justice. This includes, but is not limited to, looking at the implications of being labelled as creators or purveyors of deceptive data and the false accusations they impose despite lacking proper justifiable evidence, leading to reputational damages or unwarranted surveillance. Issues of ethics also cover the relevance and explanation of the processes and algorithms involved in disinformation detection, especially looking at who is accountable for providing these explanations. The difficulty of achieving public trust by exposing the workings of the algorithms used as a result of providing trade secrets to the public presents multi-dimensional difficulties.

Furthermore, the potential for bias—or even censorship—resulting from the multimedia training dataset and its possible misclassification of content underscores the need for vigilant counter-bias and counter-censorship measures to be in place. Additionally, the collaborative ethical concerns with government or corporate partners on disinformation detection projects highlight the need for firm boundary setting and governance to mitigate conflicts of interest that may impact the freedom of information flow and the influence of predominant narratives and analysis on the findings. As the field develops, continual conversations, cooperation across academic disciplines, and concrete ethical guidelines will be critical to the responsible evolution and application of technologies aimed at detecting disinformation. In any case, upholding ethical concerns fundamentally demonstrates a commitment to preserving core ethical principles when rising to the challenge posed by disinformation.

9

Operationalising NLP

Building, Deploying, and Managing NLP Systems in Intelligence Agencies

Understanding Agency Needs: Aligning NLP Objectives with Intelligence Goals

When comprehending agency needs, it is crucial to outline the precise intelligence needs and examine in what ways Natural Language Processing (NLP) can resolve these issues. As with other intelligence agencies, there is an unending stream of unstructured data like reports, information from social media and news sources, and communications which could provide relevant information about the nation's security posture and other policy decisions. Natural Language Processing makes it possible to streamline in dealing with large volumes of information by retrieving relevant information, recognising important patterns, and revealing pertinent intelligence. Agencies that align NLP objectives with the intelligence goals stand to enhance operational efficiency and gain timely insights on emerging threats.

Aligning intelligence goals with NLP objectives begins with analysing the specific problems pertaining to the agency. This includes appreciating the data sources, the languages in focus, the kinds of entities and events that are of interest, and the intelligence domain's contextual specifics. For example, accurate entity recognition and event extraction in multilingual communications or data collection from culturally diverse contexts. Understanding these intricacies enables tailoring of NLP-driven solutions that bolster the agency's critical intelligence operations.

NLP technology assists to a large degree with the automation of monotonous and meticulous tasks such as sorting, classifying, and summarising files of documents so that analysts can devote their full attention to sophisticated analysis as well as high-level strategic decisions. Intelligence agencies are able to swiftly transform extensive datasets into actionable intelligence products by machine learning algorithms to perform topic modelling, sentiment analysis, and information extraction on big data streams. This refinement of workflows enhances operational efficiency while allowing analysts to spend more time on demanding analytical work which leads to improved precision and speed of assessment.

Moreover, successfully integrating NLP goals with intelligence objectives involves knowing the compliance frameworks and the socio-ethical boundaries of data collection, information security, and applied AI technologies. Considerable coordination between NLP specialists, intelligence operatives, and legal and policy experts is needed to make sure that NLP technologies, while offering vital gleanings, work within legal frameworks and ethical boundaries concerning national security and defence. With regard to these considerations, NLP can be utilised to meet the intelligence requirements while ensuring transparency, accountability, and responsible innovation.

Selecting the Right Tools and Technologies: Frameworks, Libraries, and Platforms

The use of NLP involves a series of critical processes for intelligence agencies, starting with the selection of frameworks, libraries, and platforms best suited for their objectives and goals. This field of NLP frameworks, libraries, and platforms is widening by the minute, bringing unlimited choices to agencies. This document will try to highlight some of the primary considerations and best practices regarding the selection of technologies for an organisation. Choosing tool technologies starts with the needs assessment of the agency in question. Knowing what kind of information is to be processed, how much and what kinds of languages will be encountered, and the pre-existing organisational structures are key factors that shape tool selection. These factors alongside the requirements of system scalability, performance, efficiency, precision, and overall resource management during operations critically affect tool selection. Community support and integration capabilities alongside versatility are some strong additional factors to look at when dealing with NLP model frameworks like TensorFlow, PyTorch, and spaCy that already offer a strong foundation.

The libraries NLTK, Gensim, and scikit-learn offer pre-built algorithms and tools for tokenisation, part-of-speech tagging, and semantic similarity computations. Such an NLP toolkit allows agencies to accelerate model development cycles whilst preserving an expected level of quality. Further, the actual choice of systems' interfaces for the implementation of NLP technologies centres around thoughtful consideration. Vendors Amazon Web Services, Google Cloud Platform, and Microsoft Azure provide cloud-based infrastructure with easy-to-use setups for scalable and reliable NLP technology in addition to AI-powered APIs that solve difficult NLP problems automatically. Alternatives to these on-premises solutions allow clients to have strict control over data security and governance, fulfilling the needs of agencies with rigorous regulatory compliance mandates. The choice of the right set of tools, frameworks, platforms, libraries, and in combination with community support is the tactical choice that determines success on NLP projects in an intelligence agency. This has to be further weighed against technological attributes, community support, cost, and future growth potential. Having a continuous watch on the NLP technology landscape is critical to position the agency to take advantage of innovations that would improve the agency's analytical tools.

Intelligence agencies could lay a reliable groundwork in constructing, deploying, and managing Natural Language Processing systems (NLP) that correspond with their critical goals and operational workflows by methodically attending to the processes of tool and technology selection.

Building Robust NLP Models: Best Practices for Development and Training

The ability to derive valuable information from an enormous corpus of unstructured textual data forms a strategic asset for intelligence agencies and relies on properly designed natural language processing models (NLP). The development and training of NLP models requires understanding both technical and strategic considerations. We need to explain strategies that could elevate the effectiveness and accuracy of NLP models in the context of intelligence.

A deep understanding of the specific language subtleties of the area of interest is foundational. The vocabulary and grammar, including relevant contextual markers, must be thoroughly captured for domain-specific words and phrases. Such adaptations ensure that the NLP model is optimised to accurately understand and process text commensurate with the demands of intelligence analysis. Performance is also improved when specific annotated datasets from the intelligence domain are used for training and validation.

Training strategies involving pre-training phases also merit special attention, especially those that employ transfer learning with large language models such as BERT or GPT-3. Intelligence NLP systems stand to gain from the massive pre-trained models as they contain distilled knowledge that can be leveraged to understand sophisticated language used in intelligence documents and communications.

In the domain of Natural Language Processing (NLP), intelligence agency-specific data can sharpen model accuracy after pre-training, improving the recognition of subtleties in meaning and intention. Furthermore, NLP models are now capable of interpreting meanings and context within the text because of advanced feature engineering alongside text representation methods like word embeddings and contextual embeddings. This enhances the model's capability to decipher the language's deep structure and meaning—leading to improved information extraction as well as the recognition and classification of pertinent entities, sentiments, and topics in intelligence materials and documents.

These models also need to endure meticulous error analysis and iterative processes of model validation to further improve the intricacies of their design whilst adhering to robust standards of reliability. Biases, ambiguities, and other shortcomings in the model's predictions can be resolved through systematic error analysis. Moreover, performance across varied contexts of intelligence is critical, which can be ensured through rigorous methodologies such as cross-validation or benchmarking against diverse datasets.

In other words, the combination of domain know-how,

innovative techniques, and thorough compliance with defined validation benchmarks is paramount to building resilient NLP models. Adopting these practices will empower intelligence agencies to NLP systems that enhance their dynamic and multifaceted nature, deepening intelligence and refining the decision-making process.

Integration with Existing Systems: Ensuring Compatibility and Interoperability

Developing high-level NLP systems requires that they fully operate within the infrastructure and tools provided by the intelligence agencies. In this context, "integration" refers to cross-examination of elements concerning compatibility and operational standoff to enable unhindered data exchange and orchestrated work. First, the examination of the current systems is their architectural and technological stack. From this perspective, the possible integration points like APIs, data formats, and communication protocols are recognised. Systems with potential conflicts can be mapped out, and design mitigations advanced so that disruptions during integration are minimised. Also, provided decomposition needs to ensure that data exchange with other NLP system modules provides interfaces for other agents' systems as well as the NLP systems themselves, which determines the boundary security fabrication. Besides, an interface exchange boundary encapsulating other entities is critical. Also, rigorous validation of the integrated system ensures that all elements have passed the eNLP system adequacy testing in various controlled conditions without overshadowing or clashing critical operations. Documenting the active integration procedures provides metadata for processes done without losing the context for why process boundaries were drawn throughout the configuration.

Thorough documentation aids in the maintenance, updates, or changes to be made in the future within the technological scope of the intelligence agency. It is also necessary to improve inter-team collaboration as well as communication among the members dealing with various parts of the integrated systems. This approach guarantees that each participant is working towards the same goals for integration, which allows for a unified technological framework. Finally, the integration is done with close surveillance and assessment to recognise any new difficulties, areas that need optimisation, or security risks in multifunctional system components. Regular oversight helps to quickly resolve problems, so that in the end, the framework becomes agile and robust where the NLP systems enhance the capabilities of the intelligence agency.

Data Management Strategies: Ethical Sourcing, Processing, and Storage

Natural Language Processing (NLP) in intelligence agencies raises data management concerns that require scrupulous attention to detail. The ethical sourcing, processing, and storage of data within NLP functions is crucial not only for compliance with legal intelligence frameworks but also for safeguarding the integrity, privacy, and security of the information.

The ethical sourcing of data involves complying with restrictive policies on obtaining data and ensuring that it was retrieved through legal and open channels. Intelligence agencies cannot ignore the legitimacy and provenance of data sources, particularly meeting internal policies as well as external regulatory requirements. Also, intelligence agencies must have regard to the privacy rights and consent of persons whose information may be captured in the NLP data, thereby upholding confidentiality. Moreover, processing data must be ethical in all aspects, which includes responsible gathering, analysing, and transforming of information. Adequate measures to protect breaches of pseudonymisation and anonymisation on re-identification of sensitive data must be implemented.

Furthermore, extreme quality control steps have to be embedded into the processing pipeline to avert biases, errors, or discrepancies that may undermine the trustworthiness of an NLP output. With regard to data storage, agencies must implement mechanisms that are secure and compliant to enable access and retention of the data. Proactive safeguards such as encryption, data access limitations, and audit logs should be implemented to prevent exposure to unrestricted access, breaches, or tampering. Execution of retention and disposal compliances are equally important in counteracting risks of unintentionally retaining redundant data which increases vulnerability to potential litigations.

The NLP solution also must be reinforced by reliable strategies for backing up and recovering from disasters to maintain uninterrupted operation even during crises. Claiming that sensitive data is encrypted and access controlled is only true if enclaves are created to isolate that information where only vetted and cleared individuals can reach. Fostering an environment of integrity, shared governance, and thorough regulatory compliance drives the custodianship culture concerning all stages of hands-on and hands-off data processes. As discussed in the past paragraphs, the primary dealing with intelligence agencies rests on the foundations of ethical data management when implementing NLP solutions which entails harnessing technology while safeguarding the core principle of ethics and ensuring data is used responsibly to derive insights and support strategic decisions.

Deployment Architectures: Designing Scalable and Reliable Solutions

For intelligence agencies, effective Natural Language Processing (NLP) systems must be able to deploy and manage pragmatic systems that are scalable and reliable, adapting to changing operational needs. Deployment architectures are important to this and require knowledge of infrastructural design, resource allocation, system upkeep, among others. While deploying NLP systems, it is critical to attend to the requirements of intelligence analysis which necessitates expeditious processing of immense datasets of multiple strains in a secure environment with accuracy and efficiency. In order to achieve good scalability, the orchestration of computational power, network infrastructure, and storage capabilities must be tiered to an agile performance set and responsive to fluctuating workloads. Reliability, which is crucial in the context of intelligence operations, requires aggressive fault-tolerant designs, strong redundancy measures for robust business continuity, and agility in responding to disruptions or hostile actions. This goes together with additional focus areas discussed in other chapters of this book tailored for the unique concerns of intelligence agencies. With the employment of advanced cloud services, distributed computing frameworks, and containerisation technologies, analysts and system administrators are able to design solutions that are scalable and resilient, interweaving them to agilely adapt to ever-changing mission demands.

Policies regarding the integration of informatics systems are fundamentally concerned with the implementation of microservices and DevOps systems, which enhance agility and flexibility in the deployment of NLP systems. Such policies allow for new capabilities to be incorporated at an advanced pace while minimising possible system lifecycle failure points. Besides, system curing within the holistic maintenance paradigm includes performance maintaining processes such as proactive fault detection and correction, automated performance tuning, and ongoing refinement at different intervals which guarantees the system will optimise its accuracy and reliability goals over the time of its lifecycle. The realisation of deployment architecture orchestration enables intelligence agencies to fully utilise NLP systems as they provide deeply tailored and reliable, scalable, and adaptive technological insights and decision support systems for analysts.

Monitoring and Maintenance: Ensuring Performance and Accuracy Over Time

When implementing NLP systems in intelligence agencies, monitoring and maintenance stand out as core areas focusing on reliability and accuracy targeting over a prolonged period. This requires the setting up of advanced monitoring systems which supervise the active behaviour of the system, the consumption of resources, and the performance of the model in real-time. With close supervision of these areas, the agencies can ensure that issues can proactively be resolved and enhancements validated to improve optimal functionality of NLP systems.

Models in NLP technology are put to use for numerous applications and the performance of such deployed models is critical to an organisation's objectives. Measuring precision, recall, F1 scores, and model inference speed gives comprehensive insight into the effectiveness and performance of such models. Capturing user feedback along with monitoring system outputs further enables refinement of such NLP models, greatly maintaining the accuracy of such models over time.

Unlike traditional software maintenance activities, AI systems require continual maintenance such as reframing setups, updating libraries and models, putting into use the latest version of such frameworks, or even changing the model architecture in line with high-level principles from linguistics to mitigate conflicting dependencies. Components are improved and updated on a recurring schedule in order to eliminate structural flaws and keep up with the constantly evolving dynamics of language, intelligence, and the socio-political climate.

Fairness and bias mitigation measures algorithmically

are another important step in maintenance and upkeep processes. Fairness and bias audits along with retraining algorithms on wider datasets assist models in adapting to their changing environment and running devoid of violating ethical principles as mandated by our standards of fairness and anti-bias.

Despite the evolving contexts and expressions used to phrase ideas, regular curation, augmentation, and validation help datasets to remain true, relevant, and thorough.

Alongside this, effective management of the NLP systems infrastructure is critical for confidentiality and security in processing sensitive intelligence data. Routine security audits, breaches of security information monitoring, privacy by design, and strict adherence to privacy regulations constitute the maintenance framework.

To sum up, precise measures with monitoring and system maintenance have a primary focus on sustaining the performance, precision, assurance and ethical integrity of NLP systems deployed within intelligence agencies. With continuous evaluation alongside system updates, bias mitigation, and security integration, NLP infrastructures assert sustained effectiveness as well as reliability improving the agencies' analytical and strategic decision-making capabilities.

User-Centric Design: Building Interfaces for Analysts and Decision-Makers

In the context of intelligence analysis, user-centric design is vital for improving the usability and impact of NLP systems. The action tools (interfaces) through which analysts and decision makers interface with the systems impact their ability to make decisions from the available data. Therefore, here we discuss the balance between a user-centred design approach and the functional requirements of the interfacing systems within intelligence agencies.

A design which is as much as possible user-centred aims to reduce cognitive workload and enhance engagement. It demands comprehensive studies to know the most suitable requirements, conditions, likes, and dislikes of the target users. Designers can gather important contextual information concerning the use of NLP systems through user interviews, creation of personas, and user journey mapping. Also, we analyse here the dashboards and other visual representations that are meant to simplify the comprehension of deeply complex analytical results. These aids not only improve the comprehension of NLP results but also help in the rapid recognition of patterns and anomalies. Moreover, we are also concerned by the users' feedback on the relevance and correctness of the insights offered by NLP as bounded by interfaces that allow the users to comment on the workings of the system.

Continuous iterative improvement based on user evaluation is critical in ensuring the interface remains synchronised with the user's needs and workflows. Further, we aim to cover customisation and flexibility in the interface design because different users may need specific views, functions, or access levels tailored to their needs. Security aspects are integrated within the design to protect the sensitive and classified data from being accessed by unauthorised users and at the same time, make the system available to those with sufficient clearance levels. A thoughtful and purposeful user-centred design of NLP interfaces allows users, especially analysts and decision makers, to leverage on NLP technologies to extract intelligence from large volumes and diverse datasets, which enhances the strategic capabilities of intelligence agencies.

Security Protocols: Safeguarding Data and Models Against Threats

Within the bounds of an intelligence agency, the safeguarding of data and models ranks as the highest priority. The increasing use of NLP systems makes the development of effective security frameworks to protect sensitive information a necessity. This subsection will address the comprehensive protective measures that must be taken to secure NLP systems from unauthorised access, alteration, or exploitation.

In any case, it is important to lay down precise access control mechanisms. These systems should be accompanied by appropriate role assignments, access encryption, allowing only designated personnel to engage with sensitive information and NLP models through rigorous authentication frameworks. Moreover, prospective audits and reviews could assist in identifying any unusual patterns or gaps within activities and logs, leading to swift mitigation response catalysed by the identified anomalies.

Moreover, effective data protection is also ensured through role-based NLP security, which emphasises the importance of strict cohesion during information transit and rest, as well as secure algorithms. Differential privacy techniques and unique encryption algorithms can also be employed as additional measures for re-identification attack mitigations by anonymising outlined information gaps.

Model tampering brings into light another equally significant aspect: integrity of the NLP models themselves. To protect against hostile modifications of such kind, version control and digital signatures can be deployed. Given the multi-faceted nature of NLP systems, creation and deployment frameworks that provide rigorous testing systems to highlight failures would greatly improve resilience against theoretical and practical attacks.

Proactive mechanisms for threat detection and response systems are equally invaluable. Support for intrusion detection systems, anomaly detection algorithms, and behaviour analysis can help identify breaches in the system's security and suspicious activities that may compromise the normal functioning of a given system. There should also be rapid response plans and security incident response plans in place to deal with any security incidents as they occur.

As previously mentioned, personnel specifically from the given agency need to be trained so that they are able to convey the key messages that will be helpful. Training on best practices, security protocols, and risks associated with NLP systems can instil the culture of employees being guardians of the organisation's data.

If an intelligence agency implements comprehensive security protocols across all layers of the NLP systems, the agency will enhance the resilience and reliability of its NLP infrastructure, thereby assuring the protection of the data and threat mitigations.

Feedback Loops and Iterative Improvement: Continuous Learning and Adaptation

In the subject of intelligence analysis, the feedback loops, and iterative improvement are just as important as the insights themselves. Predictive analytics through

NLP systems necessitates a continual assessment mechanism so vast datasets can be processed and gleaned from in a timely manner. In regard to intelligence agencies' NLP systems, this explores the bounds and echo aspects of feedback loops and iterative improvement.

The establishment of an efficient feedback loop should involve extracting an extensive set of intelligence to and from the users, presenters, domain authorities, and system performance assessments. The intelligence systems NLP models focus on defined goals to achieve set benchmarks while effortlessly handling sentence structure and context due to the linguistic agility that has been instilled. Beyond this, strengthening the culture of constructive criticism is essential to override barriers that exist to NLP model effectiveness at temporal increments.

Iterative refinement has proven to be particularly effective in advancing NLP systems tailored for specific contexts and applications. This may also include identifying gaps that may target improving entity recognition, sentiment analysis algorithms, and topic modelling techniques. Also, human-in-the-loop systems provide contextual validation and verification, which continues to augment the quality of NLP outputs.

Adaptive NLP models necessitate the contextually active retraining of intelligence models and NLP techniques based on shifting linguistic trends and emerging context-sensitive jargon relevant to intelligence datasets. In addition, NLP models are better able to update their inference and assimilate new information as domain-specific shifts occur when machine learning techniques such as transfer learning and domain adaptation are applied.

The trade-off between a continuously evolving model and preserving tight security parameters remains a top challenge. Enabling iterative improvement to NLP systems while ensuring model accuracy demands strict safeguards to the integrity and confidentiality of classified intelligence data through the use of advanced encryption, access controls, and monitoring for anomalous behaviour within the NLP architecture.

Therefore, the integration of well-defined feedback mechanisms alongside processes of iterative refinement is vital to the ongoing development of NLP systems used in the intelligence community. Proactively adjusting and improving NLP models will greatly enhance an agency's ability to analyse and respond to shifting and multifaceted threats and a fast-changing environment.

10

The Future of NLP in Intelligence

Ethical Considerations, Emerging Trends, and Strategic Impact

Overview of NLP and Ethics

With NLP advancing alongside intelligence processes, it is important to explore the ethical considerations
that accompany this intertwining relationship. Privacy
concerns, biases built into algorithms, and transparency
are core issues of ethics that help maintain confidence
alongside responsibility in the application of sophisticated language technologies. It makes one think how
the NLP-ethics intersection challenges accepted norms
and principles of ethics within the volatility of social
changes and advanced technologies within intelligence
structures. This unit will look into the paradox of NLP's
case analytic power with NLP and violation of individual rights, social rights, and social norms. With the
NLP-ethics interaction deeply embedded, we hope to
achieve responsive-dedicated ethical paradigms in parallel to reckless innovation anchored to unyielding access,
democratic values, and human dignity.

Navigating Ethical Dilemmas: Privacy, Bias, and Transparency

Within the sphere of intelligence, natural language
processing (NLP) technologies are developing at un-

precedented speeds, raising ethical challenges of the highest importance. Out of these challenges, the intertwining complexities of privacy, bias, and accountability warrant concentrated attention. Privacy issues are at the epicentre of such factors as automated data collection and online communication mining, raising questions on information retrieval. Injunctions concerning counter-terrorism, especially in the context of a contemporary era brimming with information technology and digital traps, compel intelligence agencies to painstakingly mediate between national imperatives and privacy concerns. The intractable problem of bias in NLP also raises a critical sociocultural challenge which is capable of aggravating inequality and stigmatisation at a systems level. Mitigation of bias requires purposeful inclusion in dataset compilation, algorithmic equity, and active discrimination-free output monitoring. Furthermore, the expectations of privacy and reliability that users attribute to NLP systems motivate the disclosure of the methods constituting their derivation as well as the reasoning behind their outcomes. Such measures will not only allow the public to deem NLP acceptable, but empower it to supervise and control policy making and implementation through organised critique.

We need to ponder the implications of these ethical challenges; counter-intelligence practitioners and technologists need to look for interdisciplinary dialogues which involve philosophy, law, and social sciences. Constructive dialogue in establishing ethics, social norms, and education contributes to the responsible NLP use in counterintelligence and helps balance technological advancement and societal norm.

Regulatory Landscapes: Compliance Requirements for NLP in Intelligence

The application of Natural Language Processing (NLP) technologies in intelligence has grown in prominence, transforming how data is harnessed and analysed. There are confines and applicable rules that govern the compliance technologies, and NLP is no exception. As organisations begin utilising NLP to gain insights from previously unstructured data repositories, they must comply with numerous intertwining regulations. Let's examine the diverse compliance prerequisites related to NLP technologies in the domain of intelligence.

Primarily, the regulatory framework is fundamental for the intelligence community using NLP. Considerations such as the data protection laws, oversight of monitoring practices, and privacy regulations impose restrictions bound to affect the gathering, retaining, and computing of information, including records textually expressed and analysed through NLP models. Additionally, intelligence activities involve multi-national jurisdictions which require interfaces with numerous laws, which complicates the scenario. Moreover, compliance obligations encompass risks intertwined with outlining ethical codes beyond simple data protection such as prejudice in algorithms used for NLP, as well as accountability on the given analytical processes.

Ombudsmen have defined stipulations for various industries, which, in turn, compound the intricate layers of compliance obligations. It is crucial for intelligence officers to understand these evolving compliance obligations to manage risks and ethical dilemmas, while preserving the integrity of intelligence operations. In addition to legal and moral requirements, there is heightened focus on explainability and interpretability, especially in systems powered by artificial intelligence. Hence, intelligence operations that leverage NLP (Natural Language Processing) technologies must be bound by compliance policies that address model explainability and interpretability. Navigating and managing the web of regulations requires robust compliance policies aimed at NLP complexities in intelligence. Such policies encompass not only compliance monitoring and enforcement, but also alignment with broader risk management processes of the organisation. Intelligence agencies can transformatively leverage NLP technologies, while observing legal, ethical, and regulatory frameworks, by understanding compliance obligations and regulations and proactively resolving them.

The Role of AI Ethics Committees and Governance Frameworks

As we move through the age of new technologies and improvements in natural language processing (NLP) within intelligence operations, it is crucial to consider these changes from an ethical viewpoint which revolves around the use of such technologies. This is where the formation of committees governing the ethics of AI and policies of governance becomes pertinent. These organisations act as the stewards of ethics in NLP technologies. The committees encompass the creation of policies and principles that AI Ethics Committees will address within the intelligence community specifically confront the ethical dilemmas pertaining to NLP. These ethics committees devise strategies that resolve issues related to NLP ethics through interdisciplinary collaboration with professionals in psychology, ethics, law, and policy-making prior to their occurrence. Governance frameworks address these gaps through the provision of structural scaffolding necessary for the enforcement and application of ethical policies NLP in all areas of innovations in technologies. They also include defining processes of acquiring data, model training, algorithms and ethical audits to ensure compliance and accountability.

Moreover, these frameworks ensure inclusivity of transparency and explainability features that allow various stakeholders to grasp the reasoning behind and the results produced from NLP powered intelligence analyses. Furthermore, the AI ethics committees and governance frameworks act as proactive catalysts in nurturing public trust and confidence concerning the use of NLP technologies. Such entities engage external stakeholders, which include privacy and civil society advocates and corporate partners; as a result, there is creation of constructive feedback that co-produces ethical standards that resonate with societal values. In the end, the effectiveness of AI ethics committees and governance frameworks largely depends on how well these bodies can adapt to the rapidly changing NLP technologies. With the emergence of new capabilities and applications, these structures alongside the frameworks are obligated to constantly evaluate and redefine ethical boundaries pertaining to renewed challenges. Beyond these obligations, they have a significant duty to reshape cross-border ethical outlines, realising that the repercussions of NLP in intelligence is not restricted to one region. Fundamentally, the creation and the empowerment of such committees with governance frameworks underline a positive bottom-up approach to counterbalance brisk technological developments with robust ethics through NLP in intelligence technology that is rooted on revealing profound truths, bolstering global security and safety.

Future Trends: The Evolving Capabilities of NLP Technologies

The rise of artificial intelligence technologies and tools, like NLP, fundamentally transform intelligence in various aspects. As AI technologies are integrated into more processes, it is increasingly important to examine the ways NLP systems are developing to improve information processing and analysis. One of the leading trends toward ie-evo focuses on improving context-aware understanding. Advanced semantic models and contextual embeddings make it possible for NLP systems to interpret languages at more complex levels, hence understanding more of data. Coupled with progress towards multimodal NLPs, which entail audio, text, and visual blending, these trends mark substantial progress. Such integration enhances analysis and understanding of complicated data sets. Also, the need for explainable NLP models stems from the high-stake context of intelligence that necessitates clarity, logic, and transparency around the reasoning behind every decision taken. NLP algorithms must adapt to the greater need for human understandable rationales behind outputs, especially within sensitive intelligence frameworks.

Employing deep learning methods for NLP, such as attention mechanisms and interpretable neural networks, offers avenues for improving transparency and trust. Besides, the emergence of privacy-preserving NLP and federated learning marks an important boundary for addressing privacy concerns while utilising collective intelligence in distributed networks. This approach enables collaborative training of models while safeguarding private data. Such federated structures can therefore advance secure superintelligent operations without compromising ethical constraints. Another emerging trend is the combination of NLP with knowledge graphs and other types of structured information. NLP systems can also enrich their contextual understanding from structured datasets through graph-based reasoning which significantly enhances understanding and inferring relationships. Actionable intelligence from specialised domains is further enhanced through the incorporation of domain-specific knowledge graphs. These evolving trends will undoubtedly strengthen the foundations of intelligence analysis reshaping the field altogether as NLP technologies advance. Enabling agencies to discover sophisticated correlations and generate insights from increasingly large volumes of unstructured content explores the depths of novel discoveries.

The Effect of Quantum Computing on NLP in Intelligence

Quantum computing is on the verge of transforming natural language processing (NLP) in intelligence and espionage operations, creating novel difficulties and opportunities at the same time. These challenges arise from the powerful advantages that come with the principles of superposition and entanglement in quantum mechanics. Such a shift in the level of computation possible would revolutionise NLP work in the domain of intelligence analysis.

Arguably, one of the most pronounced changes that Quantum Computing brings about in NLP is the design of faster algorithms for the recognition of sophisticated linguistic patterns and the contextualisation of semantics. NLP models are often limited in their ability to process large volumes of unstructured text due to the reliance on classical computing architectures. Language is held up by vast permutations, and quantum algorithms such as quantum natural language processing (QNLP) seek to facilitate powerful and efficient processing of this language, thus enabling multi-layered analyses that are accurate and contextually appropriate.

Quantum computing also brings forth the ability to investigate metaphysical approaches to modelling and language representation that are beyond classical computing techniques. It is possible that quantum language models are capable of using quantum states to encode and disambiguate linguistic intricacies and ambiguities with far greater depth than what is currently accessible. The creation of quantum-enhanced language generation and translation models injects a new level of NLP that deals with expressiveness and accuracy, which causes a paradigm shift in the analytical dimensions of intelligence operations.

Yet, the uncontrolled development of quantum-powered NLP systems poses risks for data-related security, encryption, and privacy within intelligence frameworks, especially with quantum capabilities. The NLP shift employing quantum computing technology brings unrivalled processing speed, which risks established standards in cryptography, calling for new strategies in safeguarding sensitive information. The relationship between some ethical assumptions on quantum surveillance and civil liberties highlights the need for policies that seek to prevent abuse of power using advanced NLP technologies.

Essentially, the combination of quantum computing and NLP marks the dawn of a new epoch of unparalleled sophistication in intelligence analysis. Considering the various ways quantum computing can impact NLP, an intelligence agency would appreciate the strategic necessities and ethical concerns involved with the profound embracing of such a combination of technologies.

Augmented Intelligence: Human–AI Collaboration in Analytical Processes

The application of Natural Language Processing (NLP) and AI technologies has drastically altered the field of intelligence analysis. Today, it marks the beginning of collaborative, "augmented" intelligence where human analysts work cohesively with AI systems. The use of NLP and AI technologies facilitates modern machine-assisted analytical work with human analysts, who now have the ability to comb through vast troves of data aided by intricate pattern recognition and predictive modelling tasks performed by sophisticated machines. This blended method of analysis has transformed intelligence analysis by allowing for more timely and better-informed decisions that span a wide range of security issues. Augmented intelligence purportedly creates the best of both worlds by merging human reasoning with machine processing capabilities. In this case, human analysts design narratives based on context intertwined with cross-examination while AI handles documents at lightning speed, extracts meaning, and processes datasets to provide real-time analysis and AI-driven recommendations. There is a clear increasing value when human reasoning skills are added to AI functionalities as military analysis can be provided with superior AI-driven recommendations and real-time data analysis. The collaboration fosters overcoming the precision, speed, and sophistication with which the machines function to compensate for speed, greater analysis, and enhanced cognitive ability analysis. The collaboration helps resolve human shortfalls in reasoning and context-recognition nuanced gaps through human aid while mitigating those gaps through technology to provide AI logic-free systems.

Moreover, the cooperative interaction of personnel with AI systems creates evolving environments in which model training, decision support systems, and analysis are all refined through feedback. Nonetheless, the merging of human and machine capabilities raises new practical problems and ethical concerns. There must be rules defined concerning the use of AI analysis that stipulate boundaries concerning openness, accountability, and the division of obligations. The ongoing ethical discussion on augmented intelligence should also address bias, privacy, and the sensitive nature of intelligence work concerning the increased use of intelligent systems. As humans and AI systems symbiotically enhance each other in intelligence analysis, these ethical issues need to be considered with greater care and attention to detail so that the new developments in augmented intelligence do not violate principles of accuracy, justice, and human dignity. To develop a solid structure based on augmented intelligence for intelligence analysis, one will need to harness diverse knowledge from technology, ethics, governance, and intelligence to create guiding standards on the use of AI in the analysis workflow concerning its ethical boundaries.

Global Security Implications: NLP in International Intelligence Sharing

The globalisation of intelligence firmly highlights the

necessity of sharing critical international information to mitigate global security challenges. In this regard, Natural Language Processing (NLP) technologies significantly impact the global collaboration and exchange of intelligence information through their automation capabilities. Countries are empowered with NLP technologies to analyse and process vast amounts of data which is critical while dealing with thousands of languages in counterterrorism, cybersecurity, and geopolitical processes. However, the application of NLP in international intelligence sharing poses both challenges and benefits. Actively countering interpretable intelligence from various streams of languages and cultures greatly strengthens capabilities in early warning systems, threat assessment, and strategic preemptive measures. Moreover, NLP paves the way in identifying multinational networks and counteracting transnational crimes and extremist movements. Using discourse segmentation, machine translation, and sentiment analysis, NLP rudimentarily fosters statecraft by providing contextual understanding of foreign communications, thus easing diplomatic disputes and international negotiations. Nonetheless, ethics such as data privacy, information sovereignty, and possible abuse of shared intelligence strongly inform proposed international frameworks.

Managing the blend of transparency, accountability, and security in relation to the sovereignty and concerns of the participating countries is crucial. Moreover, protecting the integrity and confidentiality of shared intelligence requires protective governance structures, safe avenues for communication, and observance of applicable global laws and treaties. Overcoming these challenges, in addition to technological innovation, requires the shrewdness of diplomacy and commitment to common moral principles. Thus, the combination of NLP and international intelligence sharing highlights the need for intergovernmental agreements and cooperation, common standards, and multidisciplinary interdisciplinary frameworks to foster permanent engagement and dialogues on the responsible and ethical use of NLP for international security and the protection of humanity.

Strategic Forecasting: Preparing for Technological Shifts

With rapid advancements in any particular field, agencies of a state must be ready to adapt in anticipation of prospective changes. Contemporary foresight focuses mainly on the changes in the future setting for any particular area and their anticipated impacts. The remaining parts of this chapter are dedicated to discussing the phenomena of prospective change in the framework of NLP, its major aspects and importance, as well as infrastructure implications.

Forecasting shifts in technology requires a blend of industry insight, academic research, and advancements in computational linguistics. NLP methodologies and toolsets are of particular relevance to intelligence agencies, as emerging technologies can profoundly impact information gathering, analysis, and dissemination within the information ecosystem of the intelligence community.

Moreover, strategic forecasting refers to the assessment of new technologies that could disrupt existing workflows and infrastructure pertaining to NLP. Current systems are presumed to be profitable and effective, but those systems can quickly become out-of-date with new advancements. Predicting those changes helps streamline modernised resource allocation.

In forecasting within intelligence, there are socio-political factors and global events that are just as impactful and forecasted with equal importance. Geopolitical realignments, policy shifts, public relations regarding AI, and regulation can shift the paradigm amid intelligence analysis. Agencies that adopt these variables into their forecasting models have the capability to realign their NLP systems proactively rather than reactively, adjusting to global changes in real-time instead of waiting to adapt.

Furthermore, strategic forecasting should include concern over ethical boundaries regarding NLP technology and preemptively predicting the misuse of those boundaries. Safeguards must be in place to prevent abusive exploitation, ethical transgressions, and adversarial vulnerabilities that might accompany unregulated advancements in technology.

Fostering a culture of innovation and adaptability within intelligence agencies requires proactive strategic forecasting. Providing decision-makers and analysts with foresight capable of revealing technological trends enables agencies to continuously refine their operational budgeting and calibrate their intelligence workflows for more sophisticated NLP integration in intelligence-focused practices. Thus, strategic forecasting is foundational to assuring agility and responsiveness in adopting NLP technologies, including risk mitigation planning geared toward associated ramifications.

In the face of shifting technological paradigms in NLP, strategic forecasting stands as a distinctive exercise not only in preparedness but also an anticipatory quest for agency competitive advantage in the dynamic intelligence ecosystem. Proactively positioned to avail themselves of emerging technological opportunities, intelligence agencies will be able to leverage NLP to elevate analytic and decision-making capabilities, maintaining agility and a competitive edge within the intricate sphere of national security and intelligence.

Concluding Insights: Balancing Innovation and Accountability

As far as Artificial Intelligence (AI) technologies, especially Natural Language Processing (NLP), the industry is profoundly shifting; it is equally important to maintain accountability while balancing innovation. With fast-paced advancements sculpting the analytical landscape, practitioners and stakeholders are likely to face ethical dilemmas that require far-reaching societal considerations beyond the mere technology. The need to promote innovation while simultaneously taking responsibility conveys multilayered challenges and opportunities that require tailored strategies and frameworks.

Striking this balance requires the enforcement and application of principles of ethics considering such implications in the design and implementation stages of NLP technology is crucial. With ignoring negative consequences for poorly defined boundaries, there must be strict borders on the utilisation of NLP technologies in intelligence agencies, which in turn leads to the creation of necessary usage rules where technologies, applications, and processes incorporated by intelligence agencies undergo stringent scrutiny to ensure neutrality inertia and require transparency to whatever steps algorithmic process is quantified.

Alongside fostering a culture of accountability, it is critical to include a collective effort from technologists, ethicists, policymakers, and end-users. Meaningful dialogues and interdisciplinary collaborations harness great potential to illuminate blind spots, cultivate best practices, and foresee the NLP implementations. With the right approach, NLP in intelligence can steer towards fortifying societal values by embracing outcomes that align with the ethical fabric considering a diversity of thought and expertise.

As we strive to balance innovation and accountability, we must recognise ethics as a moving target in NLP's sphere. Framing responsive and adaptive ethical boundaries necessary for dynamic discourse on fresh NLP trends, risks, and societal impacts hinges on a constant flow of responsive discourse. NLP's burgeoning frontiers pose novel ethical dilemmas such as deep fakes, adversarial attacks, and algorithmic biases, requiring preemptive action to safeguard society from their potential harms with anticipatory responses sculpted by agile planning.

Furthermore, enforcement of responsibility along with innovation simultaneously requires implementing a steadfast organisational commitment to perpetual learning. This, in turn, aims to enrich policies on ethics shaped by actual practice as well as new regulatory developments and mandates through the NLP systems and operations skin. Along with a mindset of perpetual enhancement, intelligence practitioners can bolster the ethical resilience of NLP deployments and develop public trust and confidence by recalibrating NLP systems.

To summarise, the integration of innovation and responsibility ingrained into NLP for intelligence reflects a deep journey of self-reflection, change, and shared accountability. With the infusion of ethical boundaries, technological innovation can be directed towards an NLP-enabled future for the betterment of society and aligned with its core values. By these means, ethically sound leadership, proactive guidance, and commitment to ethical principles help balance the scales of responsibility and innovation which, in turn, enables a cohesive impact of NLP in the advancement of intelligence.